HANOI

A pocket guide to the city's best
cultural hangouts, shops, bars
and eateries

JULIETTE ELFICK

hardie grant travel

CONTENT∫

INTRODUCTION

It's 6am in Hanoi and the gentle morning light bathes the city. Its inhabitants are socialising, exercising and relaxing before the roar of motorbikes and beeping of horns take over. The parks, the roads around the lakes and the houses that open into the streets are filled with life, the pho pots full of bones and spices are put on to simmer, and fresh food and flowers are being delivered to the markets.

This is the time of day to grab your camera and try to capture something of this most photogenic of cities. Vietnamese people value aesthetics and will add beauty wherever they can. Sure there's gorgeous architecture, but there are smaller joys in the patterned paving stones, public fences, floral inlays… just look all around you.

But a camera won't capture everything there is to love about Hanoi. There's dymamic street life to join in with, the amazing tastes and smells of street food to enjoy, like bun cha (grilled pork patties) with its seductively sweet, smoky charcoal aroma, and as you learn more about the history of the place, you'll admire the spirit and resilience of the people, who have faced multiple invasions by foreign empires. The younger generation, the beneficiaries of a more open and successful economy in recent years, have travelled and brought back ideas that have re-energised the arts and cultural scenes, while maintaining a strong sense of Vietnamese pride.

Life moves at an incredible pace here, which is why it's worth rising early, like the locals, not just to photograph but to enjoy a very different Hanoi. Join in the public meandering or exercise, or in meditation sessions in public spaces, or just sitting and catching up over a green tea. You'll be prepared to get out in the fray and enjoy your day!

Juliette Elfick

A PERFECT HANOI DAY

My ideal Hanoi day starts early, at 6am, when there's no traffic and it's easy to see and photograph the beauty of Hanoi in the gentle morning light. It's when the locals are most relaxed, exercising and socialising in the parks by the lakes. I start the day in the parks along Thanh Nien, between Truc Bach and Ho Tay lakes, and watch the locals dancing, doing aerobics and catching up over a green tea.

Afterwards I head around Truc Bach Lake to Chau Long for a breakfast pho at **Pho Huyen**, then visit **Chau Long Market** and see what's fresh for the day. I like to grab a coffee at the **Hanoi Cooking Centre** and see if **Bookworm** has got some new books and browse the Vietnamese history collection upstairs.

I'll take a taxi to the **Vietnamese Women's Museum** to see their latest exhibition, then have lunch at **Chim Sao** or **Nha Hang Ngon** for delicious Hanoi and regional cooking. Afterwards I wander down to **Café Mai** for a heart-starting Vietnamese coffee to ready myself for the craziness of the Old Quarter. I head up past Hoan Kiem Lake to Hang Dau, then get lost in the busy streets and eventually find my way to **Tan My Design** for some high-end shopping, then poke around in nearby outlet shops for some adventure-wear bargains.

I like to meander south through the little lanes until I reach the faded beauty of **St Joseph's Cathedral** and do some shopping at **Chula** and **Collective Memory** on Nha Chung, then at the boutiques on Nha Tho.

By now it's time for a break so I take a taxi out to Tay Ho for a well-deserved massage at **Yakushi**, followed by a juice on the lakeside rooftop at **Oriberry** across the road. I'll take a stroll around the grand villas of Tay Ho, winding up at the beautiful temple **Phu Tay Ho**. After exploring the temple grounds I'll walk through the lovely neighbourhood along the lake road to **Don's Bistro** for a sunset drink, then head up the road to **Bia Hoi Nha Hang 68** for some excellent Vietnamese grilled meats and salads, washed down with bia hoi (street beer). If I'm still up for going back into town, I head down to Tong Duy Tan for a drink at railway line bar **Ray Quan** (making sure that on the way I go past Ba Dinh Square to see the **Ho Chi Minh Mausoleum** lit up) in time to watch the evening train to Sapa roar past. Afterwards, the perfect way to finish the perfect Hanoi day – a classy nightcap and a bit of late-night jazz at the **Metropole**.

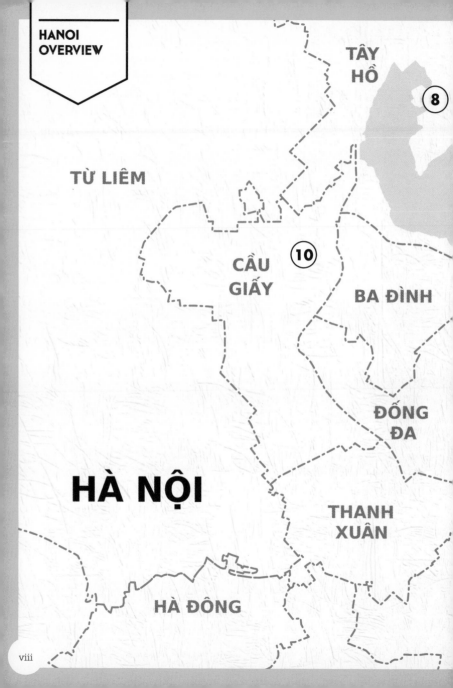

8

TÂY HỒ

TỪ LIÊM

CẦU GIẤY

10

BA ĐÌNH

ĐỐNG ĐA

HÀ NỘI

THANH XUÂN

HÀ ĐÔNG

ĐÔNG
ANH

LONG
BIÊN

HOÀN
KIẾM

HAI BÀ
TRƯNG

HOÀNG MAI

GIA
LÂM

PRECINCTS

1. Old Quarter
2. South of Hoan Kiem
3. Hai Ba Trung
4. Nha Tho
5. Tong Duy Tan
6. Greater Ba Dinh and Surrounds
7. Ba Dinh – Truc Bach
8. Tay Ho – Quang An
9. Tay Ho – Nghi Tam

FIELD TRIPS

10. Vietnam Museum of Ethnology
11. Halong Bay
12. Bat Trang
13. Sapa

OLD QUARTER

Every now and then in Hanoi you meet someone who grew up in the Old Quarter, and they'll tell you stories of living in traditional long tube houses with shopfronts, chasing chickens around the carless streets, visiting temples with family, daily shops at the market – a life which rarely involved leaving the area. It's a snapshot of a life that is fast disappearing in Hanoi, but it's one you can still get a glimpse of in the Old Quarter if you spend a bit of time there.

Some visitors can find the Old Quarter too claustrophobic and frenetic – which is why I never recommend that first-time visitors stay there – but once you're used to the pace it's a fascinating place, full of life. The area is often called 'the 36 streets' because of the 36 craft guilds that were based there and whose names adorn the streets – if a street name starts with 'Hang' it is one of these streets. There are actually more than 36 streets in the Old Quarter, an area that for the purposes of this book stretches from the north end of Hoan Kiem Lake over to the dyke road in the east and north, all the way to Phung Hung in the east. The area nearest to the lake is the most tourist-oriented, with Hang Be and Ma May featuring travel agencies and Western-style cafes and restaurants. As Ma May turns into Hang Buom it becomes a backpacker haven, stretching to the bar street of Ta Hien. Wander further north to find Dong Xuan market and the great street food in the alleyway behind it. From here to the west, the Old Quarter is a quieter, more relaxed place, where you can happily get lost for a couple of hours.

→ *Bach Ma Temple – a hidden spiritual oasis*

1

1 BACH MA TEMPLE

76 Hang Buom
Open Mon–Sun 8–11am &
2–5pm
[MAP p. 181 B3]

Walking into Bach Ma
(White Horse) temple from
the busy streets outside is
a magical experience – it's
quiet and dark; elaborate
red and gold lacquerwork,
paintings, colourful flags and
religious ornaments fill the
space, softened by occasional
greenery. Hidden behind the
modest yellow exterior, found
right in the middle of the
Old Quarter, the temple is said
to be Hanoi's oldest. There are
a number of ancestral altars
filled with offerings but the
main altar is dedicated to the
white horse that helped the
king (and founder of Hanoi)
Ly Thai To decide where
to build the temple in the
11th century. There are some
intricate architectural details
on the smaller buildings and
altars around the sides of the
temple. Spend some time in
here – give yourself time to
soak in the grandeur of this
beautiful temple.

2 NGOC ſON TEMPLE

Dinh Tien Hoang
Open Mon–Sun 8am–5pm
[MAP p. 175 E2]

In a city full of beautiful temples and pagodas, Ngoc Son Temple is the one most tourists will visit or at least see as they pass Hanoi's most famous attraction, Hoan Kiem Lake. This means it can be pretty crowded, so before you pay your entry fee and cross the red wooden bridge, have a look at the crowds.

Ngoc Son is a Buddhist temple that sits on the small island on the north-east side of Hoan Kiem Lake, known as the Jade Island. The temple consists of two connected structures – the one facing north is dedicated to heroes General Tran Hung Dao and saint Van Xuong. The tall tower is Pen Tower, dedicated to Confucian scholar Nguyen Van Sieu, which is why you see students coming here to pray for good marks. Look out for the huge embalmed turtle, sadly the only kind you'll see around here since the lake's much-loved sacred turtle died in 2016. The gift shop is quite good and worth a look, and the beautiful gardens are nice to relax in.

3 LY THAI TO PARK & SQUARE

Dinh Tien Hoang
[MAP p. 175 F4]

Hanoi's definitely a 'work hard, play hard' kind of place, and it's good fun to come to Ly Thai To Park and see the locals kick back after hours (or you can even join in the fun). At nights and on weekends, Ly Thai To Park is filled with activity – agile oldies doing ballroom dancing or tai chi moves, kids whizzing around in circles on two-wheeled, self-balancing hoverboards (which you can often hire in the park if you're brave), and teenagers jiving to a live swing band.

The park sits on the eastern side of Hoan Kiem Lake, watched over by the imperious statue of Ly Thai To, who, as king, founded the city in 1010 when he chose this spot on the banks of the Red River to be his capital. On weekends when the road between the park and Hoan Kiem Lake is closed to traffic you can enjoy a view of the lake .

4 TAN MY DE/IGN

61 Hang Gai
3825 1579
www.tanmydesign.com
Open Mon–Sun 8am–8pm
[MAP p. 174 C1]

If the chaos of trying to shop in hot, cramped, dimly lit stores is getting to you, pay a visit to Tan My Design. It's the nearest the Old Quarter gets to a plush department store, complete with a very cool cafe/gallery (check out the giant ant sculptures crawling down one wall) that serves coffee and, if you're feeling like a bit of luxury, champagne. If you don't have a lot of time to shop it's also a one-stop shop where you can buy the best of Hanoi's upmarket clothing, art, jewellery, homewares and souvenirs. Most items are expensive but there are some bargains in there.

It is worth exploring the whole of the store, as each new floor holds new and different products, and to be honest, it's just nice sometimes to shop in Hanoi in a pristine, ordered, airy environment. Tan My Design occupies a huge building and dominates the exclusive silk boutiques in the middle of the Old Quarter's silk street, Hang Gai. Local designers are showcased, including Ipa-Nima (see p. 51) and Valerie Cordier handbags, Chula (see p. 52) and Future Traditions (see p. 123), as well as the Vietnamese fragrance line Cochine.

5 DONG XUAN MARKET

Dong Xuan
3828 2170
www.dongxuanmarket.com.vn
Open Mon–Sun 6am–6pm
[MAP p. 181 B3]

Dong Xuan Market is similar to many other markets in Asia that sell anything that's cheap and cheerful, manufactured in Vietnam or other nearby Asian countries – plastic hairbands, fake watches, kitchen implements, toys, you name it … but what this market does really well is fabrics. Upstairs is packed with every kind of fabric you might want – from stretchy t-shirt material to silk and linen, it rivals Cho Hom (p. 42) as the place to buy fabric in Hanoi. The spice and dried food section is also worth a visit and will teach you a lot about the basics of Vietnamese cooking. From the more recognisable star anise and cassia bark (like cinnamon) to more unusual annatto seeds, dried squid, bamboo and tofu, many elements of Vietnamese cooking are here. If it all gets too much, have a seat at the counter of the drinks stand on the ground floor – it sells fresh coconut drinks and snacks – or head down the street on the south side of the market towards the back of the market and turn right into a street-food alley, one of Hanoi's best street-food areas.

6 HANOI HERITAGE HOUƧE & HANOIA

87 Ma May
6293 6087
www.hanoia.com
Open Mon–Sun 8am–9pm
[MAP p. 181 C4]

Hanoi Heritage House is an example of an old-style Hanoian 'tube' house – long and thin with a central courtyard. Here, for 10,000VND, you can see how Hanoians lived in the 19th century. The family that originally lived here would have lived at the back and had a shop at the front. This tradition has been cleverly replicated with a small boutique selling artisan-quality lacquerware with a modern take on the more classic but quickly and cheaply produced dark lacquer paintings and tableware you see everywhere in Hanoi. Hanoia's craftsmanship and design using modern, brightly-coloured objects is a revelation – a sky blue canister adorned with a gold character on it, simple bold geometric jewellery designs, or a rectangular jewellery box adorned with stencil art. It's sophisticated, sleek design that takes a traditional craft and updates it beautifully.

7

7 NIGHT MARKET

Hang Dao
Open Fri–Sun from 7pm
[MAP p. 181 B4]

Visit Hanoi's night market not so much for what you can buy – the usual t-shirts, toys, sunglasses, souvenirs, mobile-phone covers – but for the buzz of people-watching, stopping every now and then for a beer or snack, seeing everyday Hanoians reclaiming the closed-off Old Quarter streets at night. It's fairly safe and hassle free (though, as with other markets, keep an eye on your wallet), so it's family friendly and you'll see locals with kids visiting the market late into the night. Bargaining is accepted at most places so give it a try, though don't be surprised if you're just completely ignored at some stalls. If you are there to shop, the best buys are the always-popular Apple parody 'I-Pho', or t-shirts printed with tangled electricity wires, as well as silk table runners and purses.

8 GINKGO

44 Hang Be
3926 4769
www.ginkgo-vietnam.com
Open Mon–Sun 8am–10pm
[MAP p. 181 C4]

Ginkgo specialises in the kind of cool, often ironic, graphic depictions of traditional Vietnamese symbols that are so popular with young Hanoians right now. Ginkgo products feature some of the best iconography of the city – shirts stamped with the phone numbers you see painted on walls (they're advertisements for tradespeople) or little plastic stools, coasters featuring overloaded motorbikes, notebooks featuring covers with birds in cages – if you've seen it in Vietnam, Ginkgo's made a stylised graphic image of it and used it on one of their creations. They also sell a range of kids clothes and some stores sell old-fashioned Vietnamese games. Check out the cards featuring 'bad historical characters in Vietnam'. Other store locations can be found at 79 Hang Gai and 35 Ta Hien.

9 SHOE STREET

Lo Su & Hang Dau
[MAP p. 175 E2]

If you've brought your best pair of shoes with you to Hanoi, one of your first stops should be to 'shoe street' to buy a couple of pairs of cheap, high-soled shoes. Between having glue melt in your soles on hot days, uneven roads and footpaths breaking heels, or having to wade through rivers of water after summer storms, if you are walking around Hanoi, there's a good chance your shoes will end up worse for wear! The solution is to do as the locals do and get some cheap, hard wearing rubber slides that will withstand all kinds of weather and can be removed easily (especially if you are going inside temples and people's houses). Besides, it's quite good fun to look at the variety of shoes here – blingy high heels, imitation Chanel-branded brogues and squeaky kids shoes. There are usually shoes in larger sizes, but if you're out of luck, head down to Vincom Towers (*see* p. 41) in Ha Ba Trang where you'll find all the international brands (but you'll have to pay a lot more).

POCKET TIP

Around the corner from Lo Su, just past the water puppets at the top of Hoan Kiem Lake, there's a row of luggage shops that sell brands like Kipling and Fjallraven Kanken.

10 TRANQUIL BOOKS & COFFEE

5 Nguyen Quang Bich
0989 38454
Open Mon–Sun 8am–10.30pm
[MAP p. 181 A4]

Tranquil Books & Coffee is like that comfy cafe back home where you can you curl up on a sofa for hours, reading a book, or making good use of the wi-fi and no one bothers you. Confusingly there are two branches of this cafe on the same crooked little street just north of the Old Quarter – one faces directly onto the street and the second, almost opposite, is tucked away in a little lane on a slight bend in the road. Look for the sign out front, walk down the lane into the courtyard, and then into the cafe. Inside, a massive bookshelf dominates the room, there's a piano, some sofas, tables and chairs scattered about and an old black-and-white photo of John Lennon hanging above the fireplace. The staff are young and don't speak much English, but are friendly. Food choices are limited to sweet options but it's the atmosphere here (and maybe the free wi-fi) that you'll like and it's a good place to spend a few hours while sipping on a coconut coffee. At night they sometimes have musical performances – see the Facebook page (cafetranquil) for more details.

11 BANH CUON GIA TRUYEN THANH VAN

12 Hang Ga, Hang Bo
3828 0108
Open Mon–Sun 7am–1pm &
5–11pm
[MAP p.181 A3]

It's not often you can say you've just had a totally new food experience. This banh cuon (filled rice noodle sheets) restaurant is one of the few places in Hanoi where you can try ca cuong essence, a weirdly sweet-tasting liquid, extracted from the Lethocerus Indicus beetle. A small drop of this essence is added to banh cuon sauce to create a flavour that's quite hard to describe – some say it's like rock candy, which explains why kids used to suck the essence out of the beetle. Order the banh cuon with this sauce and a waiter will come to show you a tiny little bottle containing a clear liquid and add it to the banh cuon dipping sauce.

The restaurant has been recently renovated and expanded due to its growing success; it's an efficient, clean, bright place that only serves a few dishes, like a street-food vendor, but the banh cuon are light and practically melt in your mouth. Options for stuffings include pork and prawn banh cuon; portions are small so order up!

12 XOI YEN

35B Nguyen Hu Huan
3926 3427
Open Mon–Sun 7am–11pm
[MAP p. 181 C4]

Xoi Yen specialises in one dish – sticky rice, or 'xoi' – that is served with a variety of delicious toppings and can be eaten at any time of day. It's incredibly addictive, cheap (30,000 to 50,000VND) and filling. It makes a great breakfast alternative to the usual pho and you'll see street vendors selling their versions of it at breakfast time, though theirs doesn't come with the scrumptious toppings served here. Xoi Yen's sticky rice is mixed with oil and can also come with white corn and fried shallots. Then toppings are added, including soy-braised pork belly (the best!), poached chicken, tofu, lap cheong sausage, pork floss and boiled eggs. An unusual, very Vietnamese topping is the roast cinnamon pork, which is a pork paste flavoured with cinnamon and shaped into a loaf, which is then sliced. The restaurant itself is pretty basic, with low tables and stools; staff don't speak English, though there are English-language menus. You can have a look at the toppings in the open kitchen and point at what you want. Kids usually love this food as well as the cold bottles of sweet soy milk they serve.

13 NEW DAY

72 Ma May
3828 0315
www.newdayrestaurant.com
Open Mon–Sun 10am–9pm
[MAP p. 181 C4]

When a restaurant is smack bang in the middle of the most touristy areas of Hanoi, I'd normally avoid it, but when your Vietnamese friends tell you it's where they go for com bin danh (Vietnamese buffet) you know you have to try it. New Day is air-conditioned, clean and comfortable, and has really good food. It is unusual for this street that a restaurant is frequented equally by locals and tourists – locals mostly in the morning, who like the sanitised version of com bin danh, and tourists at night. The flurry of uniformed young staff don't speak much English but there is an English-language menu or you can head to the buffet in the room next door and point to what you'd like. Try the set menu for 125,000VND for four dishes including pho, local spring rolls and a main dish with rice and yoghurt, which is excellent. You can also order Vietnamese classics from the menu such as barbecued pork ribs (125,000VND), chicken with lemongrass (85,000VND) and grilled eggplant (45,000VND), washed down with a Hanoi beer.

14 BANH MI 25

25 Hàng Cá
0977 668895
Open Mon–Sun 7am–5pm
[MAP p. 181 B3]

The slick modern branding of this street cart banh mi joint hides the fact that this has been a family business for over 70 years, with all ingredients made from scratch. It's a little out of the main action of the Old Quarter but worth the walk to get your hands on the excellent banh mi (Vietnamese-style baguettes filled with deli meats, pickled vegetables and herbs). The banh mi cart serves as a mini kitchen and sits in front of a traditional tube house, where young staff in Banh Mi 25 t-shirts quickly take and fill the orders of the waiting line. Fillings include pork, chicken, pâté, egg, cheese and tofu or you can get a mixed one for 25,000VND. There's an inside area where you can sit, eat and drink beer or iced tea under fans.

15 CHA CA LA VONG

14 Cha Ca
3823 9875
Open Mon–Sun 11am–2pm
& 5.30–9pm
[MAP p. 181 B3]

You'd think producing the same dish for over 140 years would get a bit boring for the Doan family, but lucky for us, they're happy to keep churning out their scrumptious fried catfish dish day after day. Open since 1871, Cha Ca La Vong is said to be Hanoi's oldest restaurant. Its dark, cramped, slightly shabby interior certainly feels like it, however you come here for the one dish it serves, cha ca – dill and spring onions cooked with turmeric-marinated catfish, served with noodles, peanuts and fresh herbs. It's an unusual dish full of lots of interesting flavours, and it is fast becoming popular outside of Vietnam, but it's worth coming here for an authentic version of it. Due to the limited menu and open flames on each table, this is not a good place to take small children. If you can't make it here, make sure you try this dish at least once – fairly decent versions of cha ca can be ordered at some other Vietnamese restaurants around town such as Quan An Ngon (*see* p. 32) and Nha Hang Ngon (*see* p. 31).

16 NAM BITTET (BIT TET HAI TY)

20 Hang Giay
0904 339704
Open Mon–Sun 5–10.30pm
[MAP p. 181 B3]

After days of eating Vietnamese noodle soups and salads, sometimes you just crave a bit of comfort food from back home. That's the perfect time to try the Vietnamese version of steak – bit tet – thin steak served in gravy with either potato or sweet potato chips and banh mi. Nearby Hoe Nhai in Ba Dinh has a street of bit tet restaurants but I prefer this place in a quiet little corner of the Old Quarter, particularly after a lazy afternoon at a bia hoi (street beer) stall on nearby Ta Hien. This street corner is not too noisy but there's enough action around to enjoy a bit of people-watching – locals gossiping, motorbike parking attendants trying to park three bikes where only two should go and the odd roaming chicken wandering by. Two shirtless, tattooed, muscular chefs cook at barbecues on a nearby rooftop, their antics and the spectacle of the flames entertaining the diners. Almost everyone orders either the roast pigeon or steak and chips, which come with banh mi and a cucumber salad. Be warned, the roast pigeon comes with its head still on – not for the squeamish!

17

17 CAFE PHO CO

11 Hang Gai
3928 8153
Open Mon–Sun 8am–11pm
[MAP p. 175 D1]

Hanoi is full of 'hidden gems', some a bit too well hidden, such as Cafe Pho Co, a place where Hanoians come for the view of Hoan Kiem Lake and the house specialty, egg coffee. Egg coffee, or cap phe trung, is made with whipped egg yolk, and tastes a bit like tiramisu. To find Cafe Pho Co, walk through the silk shop at 11 Hang Gai, down the narrow hallway and into the courtyard of this classic ancient-style house. Check out the artwork and knickknacks and say hello to the rooster while you give your order before heading up to the third floor. There's an incredible family altar on the second floor as you head up, and one of the best views of Hoan Kiem Lake from the third floor. It's a long way up quite narrow stairs, so if it's too much trouble, settle at the mezzanine floor overlooking the courtyard; there's no lake view, but it's perfect for taking in the charms of this beautiful old building.

18 HIGHWAY 4

5 Hang Tre
3926 4200
www.highway4.com
Open Mon–Sun
10.30am–11.30pm
[MAP p. 181 C4]

As with every Highway 4 restaurant, this branch of the very successful chain is beautifully decorated (check out their woven fish net lampshades) and their huge menu has interesting regional foods such as snail meatloaf (tastes a bit fishy), and plainer dishes if you're not feeling adventurous! The dish I have to order every time is their signature dish, catfish spring rolls, crispy fried catfish and dill rolled together in rice paper and served with a moreish secret sauce. It's a little pricier than many other Vietnamese places but it's worthwhile considering the beautiful surroundings, consistent quality, cleanliness and generally relaxing atmosphere. Vietnamese people come here to drink, so if a large group comes in it might be a little noisy. Join in and order from the Son Tinh rice wines, some of the finest around.

19 COM QUE DINH LIET

40 Dinh Liet
3926 0798
Open Mon–Sun 9am–9pm
[MAP p. 175 D1]

Com bin danh is a Vietnamese buffet, usually featuring 10 or more dishes served with rice, often eaten by workers at lunchtime. This place is one of the best com binh danh in Hanoi, which means a high turnover, so the food is fresh and hasn't been sitting out in extreme heat for too long. It's a good opportunity to try different Vietnamese dishes, it's cheap and you can order by pointing at dishes that take your fancy. Anything that looks like pork or chicken is usually good, and tofu dishes are also pretty flavoursome (though not necessarily vegetarian). If you're adventurous, try the silkworms. Service here comes with a grunt and not so much eye contact, but it's quick. The dining room has no aircon or wi-fi. Still, with a wide range of Vietnamese dishes to try at 60,000 to 100,000VND for two dishes with rice, or around 30,000VND per dish, it's worth a visit. You'll find it at the start of a little street just north of Hoan Kiem Lake.

POCKET TIP

On the weekends, the Museum of Ethnology (*see* p. 146) has water-puppet shows in a small pond in its park several times a day.

20 THANG LONG WATER PUPPETS

57b Dinh Tien Hoang
0424 38249494
www.thanglongwaterpuppet.org
[MAP p. 175 E1]

The Thang Long Water Puppets seems to really divide people – if you normally like puppet shows and like world music, you'll probably like it, if not, maybe skip it. This traditional Vietnamese puppet performance is an artform unique to northern Vietnam – it features a pool of water for a stage with puppeteers hidden behind a screen. It was first performed in rice paddies where hidden puppeteers would be waist-deep in water. Traditional musicians and singers and ornate sets bring to life legends often about aspects of rural life, such as the rice harvest.

The performances are in Vietnamese but, much like a Punch-and-Judy show, the slapstick nature of the comedy and over-the-top performances can still be enjoyed by non-Vietnamese speakers. Kids will love it, and it's an inexpensive and fun place to spend an hour cooling down and resting after a foray into the Old Quarter. On your way into the theatre be sure to pick up an English-language leaflet explaining the performances.

SOUTH OF HOAN KIEM

The streets south of Hoan Kiem are a mixture of refined colonial grandeur and more modern, functional buildings. Trang Tien is an elegant boulevard that starts at the Opera House, brushes the south end of Hoan Kiem Lake and heads west, changing names every now and then as it goes. Ngo Quyen is home to the timeless glamour of the Metropole, then as it heads south, is lined with multi-storey office buildings, banks and luxury stores.

During the week it's as busy as the downtown of a city should be, and the beauty and tranquility of Hoan Kiem Lake is muted by the roar of traffic on the roads ringing its banks. But on the weekends, when the roads surrounding the lake are closed, the area becomes a wonderfully relaxing leisure space for Hanoians of all ages. A group of grandmothers does aerobics to loud techno outside the striking post office building on Dinh Tien Hoan, wealthy Hanoians kick back in the cafes around the Hanoi Opera House and police try to control the crowds of teenagers on scooters trying to get an ice cream at Kem Trang Tien.

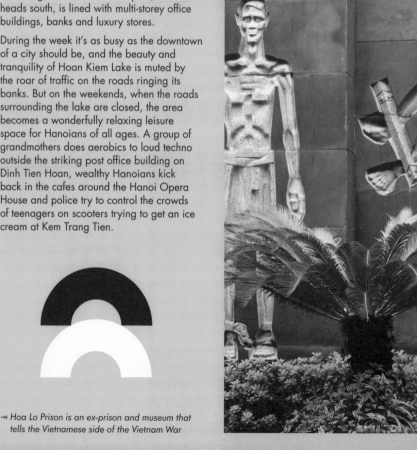

→ *Hoa Lo Prison is an ex-prison and museum that tells the Vietnamese side of the Vietnam War*

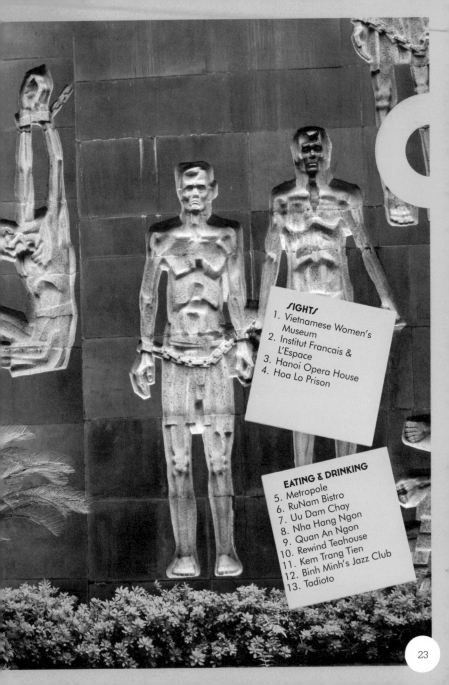

SIGHTS
1. Vietnamese Women's Museum
2. Institut Francais & L'Espace
3. Hanoi Opera House
4. Hoa Lo Prison

EATING & DRINKING
5. Metropole
6. RuNam Bistro
7. Uu Dam Chay
8. Nha Hang Ngon
9. Quan An Ngon
10. Rewind Teahouse
11. Kem Trang Tien
12. Binh Minh's Jazz Club
13. Tadioto

1 VIETNAMESE WOMEN'S MUSEUM

36 Ly Thuong Kiet
3825 9936
www.baotangphunu.org.vn
Open Mon–Sun 8am–5pm
[MAP p. 179 A1]

If you had to choose just one museum to visit in central Hanoi, this is the one. It's hard to come to Vietnam without thinking of the war in the 1970s, which inspired many a Hollywood film, but what these films don't often show is the story from the Vietnamese perspective and the pivotal role that female soldiers played in this conflict. The Vietnamese Women's Museum tells many of their stories in pictures, sharing the lives of women in various parts of Vietnamese society, from traditional wedding ceremonies, farmers and ethnic minority women, to female soldiers and warriors throughout Vietnamese history. The propaganda posters around the gallery are a graphic designer's dream and some are for sale in the excellent gift shop in the foyer. Entry is 30,000VND, and it's recommended to get the audio tour for 30,000VND.

POCKET TIP

Hai Ba Trung street and area were named after the two Trung sisters who led the military against Chinese invaders around 40AD.

2 INSTITUT FRANCAIS & L'ESPACE

24 Trang Tien
3936 2164
www.institutfrancais-vietnam.com/category/hano
Open Mon–Sun 9.30am–7pm
[MAP p. 179 B1]

Step in from busy Trang Tien and enjoy the sanctuary of this quiet, cool and modern space. On the right-hand side is an art exhibition space, and on the left, just past reception, is a small branch of the French cafe chain St Honore, complete with excellent buttery pastries, patisserie-level cakes and hot food, as well as good Western-style coffee. Up the central staircase is the auditorium where a diverse array of cultural events take place, including music concerts, films and dance. The website lists upcoming events in French and Vietnamese for the L'Espace performance space; for English-language listings, check cultural events website www.hanoigrapevine.com. The upper floors contain the Institut Francais French language school and library – if you're in the building during class changeover time, be prepared to be bowled over by students rushing in and out.

3 HANOI OPERA HOUSE

1 Trang Tien
3933 0133
www.hanoioperahouse.org.vn
Open Mon–Sun 8am–5pm
(sometimes only open during
performance times)
[MAP p. 179 C1]

It's a surreal moment when you
first step inside the auditorium
of the Hanoi Opera House
and experience its ornate,
grand, very un-Vietnamese
interior. Built by the French
between 1901 and 1910 and
carefully refurbished in 1997,
it was inspired by the Charles
Garnier–designed Paris opera
house. The performance
space is not big enough to
stage a full opera, but instead
features performances by
foreign and local classical and
folk musicians, opera singers
and ballet companies. After
the show, if the front rooms
upstairs are open to the public,
venture onto the balconies,
which have a spectacular
view down Trang Tien,
Hanoi's grandest boulevard
and a reminder of the French
influence in Hanoi's town
planning. Then scoot over to
the Metropole (*see* p. 28) for a
drink. Don't worry too much
about dressing up, but it's
fun to do.

POCKET TIP
If the Vietnamese
acrobatic troupe Lune
Productions is performing,
theirs are must-see,
thrilling shows.

4 HOA LO PRISON

1 Hoa Lo
3934 2253, 3824 6358
Open Mon–Sun 8–11.30am
& 1.30–5pm
[MAP p. 178 B1]

Dubbed the Hanoi Hilton by American prisoners of war (POWs) during the Vietnam War, this prison's most famous inmate (in the West) was American politician John McCain, who has described his horrific experience here in a book called *Faith of My Fathers*. However, the exhibition you will see here today focuses more on the Vietnamese prisoners and their treatment by the French. The site is just a small part of the original prison, but there's a diorama to show you what the whole place once looked like. Some parts of the prison are quite grisly and depressing, notably the stockade room, dungeon and guillotine. Luckily, for some relief there is a beautiful memorial garden honouring Vietnamese revolutionaries outside. Be aware that some people who are only familiar with the Western version of the events during the Vietnam War can find Hoa Lo prison quite confronting.

5 METROPOLE

15 Ngo Quyen
3826 6919
www.sofitel-legend-metropole-
hanoi.com
[MAP p. 179 B1]

The Metropole's the place to
treat yourself when the buzz of
Hanoi all gets a bit much. It's a
classic Hanoi landmark – the
building is a refined, beautifully
maintained example of French
colonial architecture, and it
has a luxurious in-house spa,
high-end shops and Italian and
Chinese restaurants. The most
accessible part is Le Club bar
in the hotel's atrium where
you can gaze out at the pool
or people-watch as soft jazz
music plays (there are live
performances on weekend
evenings). The food and
drinks are pricey but excellent
and beautifully presented
and served. My favourite is
the Graham Greene, named
after one of the many foreign
luminaries who have visited
or stayed here; others include
Noël Coward, Charlie Chaplin
and W. Somerset Maugham,
and, later (and controversially
during the Vietnam War), Jane
Fonda and Joan Baez.

POCKET TIP

During the day Vietnamese
brides and grooms pose
for photos nearby, often
across the road, in an
effort to capture the
Metropole building in
the background.

6 RUNAM BISTRO

6 Phan Chu Trinh
3934 6346
Open Mon–Sun 7am–11pm
[MAP p. 179 C1]

RuNam Bistro is the elegant new kid on the block in this upscale strip next to the Hanoi stock exchange and opposite the Hanoi Opera House (*see* p. 26). Part of a chain, RuNam also has a cafe in Nha Tho, but it's this location that really pulls together upmarket interior design that feels plush without being generic and boring. Upstairs is a little terrace from where you can watch the action near the opera house and the gardens opposite. The food is a fairly pricey mix of Vietnamese and Western food, so try the desserts and something off the extensive drinks menu and enjoy watching Hanoi's well-heeled relax. Do as they do and try the RuNam Tea Sets (195,000VND); you get a pot of tea with a small selection of Vietnamese treats such as peanut candy and green bean cakes.

7 UU DAM CHAY

34 Hang Bai
0981 349898
www.uudamchay.com/en
Open Mon–Sun 7am–10pm
[MAP p. 179 B2]

Set in a modern villa with
endless, airy dining rooms, a
beautiful terrace and a bar,
Uu Dam Chay manages to
be both elegantly stylish and
quietly spiritual at the same
time. Monks, business people
and ladies who lunch all
come here to enjoy the very
photogenic, healthy vegan
and vegetarian dishes. The
design is both cutting edge
and calming – natural products
such as bamboo, driftwood
and hanging plants are paired
with industrial chic–polished
concrete, patterned tiles and
contemporary lights – to create
a stylish but very peaceful
oasis. The dishes are really
unusual. The lotus chips
are a must, as are the girdle
cakes (large rice crackers from
central Vietnam topped with
mushrooms and tofu), fresh
spring rolls and the mushroom
hotpot, washed down with the
refreshing brown rice tea.

8 NHA HANG NGON

26A Tran Hung Dao
3933 6133
Open Mon–Sun 8am–11pm
[MAP p. 179 C2]

Nha Hang Ngon is one of those places that makes me remember why I love Hanoi – an extensive menu of reasonably priced Vietnamese dishes served up in a spectacular setting. A covered courtyard hung with twinkling fairy lights sits between two grand yellow villas. You can sit outside or in one of the many dining rooms in the villas. It's one of those rare restaurants loved by locals and tourists alike, and its dishes are faithful renditions of Hanoian and regional Vietnamese dishes, so you can sample a real variety of food. Popular dishes include bun cha (barbecue pork with noodles), xoi (sticky rice with mung beans), cha ca (turmeric and dill catfish) and boi ot (chargrilled beef chunks dipped in lime and chilli salt) – a deceptively simple but unmissable dish. Most staff don't speak English but the menu is in English and Vietnamese.

9 QUAN AN NGON

18 Phan Boi Chau
3942 8162/3
Open Mon–Sun 11am–11pm
[MAP p. 177 E4]

Quan An Ngon serves a sanitised version of Hanoi's famous street food and some regional food, and that's not such a bad thing; their versions of these foods are really very tasty and pretty authentic. There's a happy, bustling atmosphere in the large courtyard, beautifully decorated with lanterns, sheltering an easy mix of local Vietnamese, expats and tourists. The large menu at Quan An Ngon means you can come back night after night and try different food, ticking off specialty dishes you might otherwise have had to trek around the Old Quarter for ages to find. Here you'll find street-food favourites such as banh xeo (stuffed turmeric pancakes), bun bon nam bo (beef noodle salad), banh tom (sweet potato and prawn fritters) and bun rieu (crab and tomato soup). It's a good place to try Vietnamese desserts (che), which often contain coconut milk and shaved ice – so refreshing!

10 REWIND TEAHOUSE

11B Hang Khay
0868 609930
Open Mon–Sun 9am–11pm
[MAP p. 179 B1]

Every tourist guide has a favourite cafe with a view over Hoan Kiem Lake – usually it's at the northern end of the lake, but the southern end is an altogether quieter, gentler experience. From Rewind Teahouse the lake view includes leafy trees and parkland. Run by a group of committed young Vietnamese Anglophiles inspired by the tearoom at Liberty's in London, every element of Rewind Teahouse has been thought through to reflect the owners' love of traditional British afternoon teas, including importing Cornish clotted cream, and teaching local staff about the ritual and tastes of a true British afternoon tea. Scones with Cornish clotted cream and jams from Dalat is 85,000VND; you can eat these with any upmarket tea from Twinings or Whittards, or you can go for the full tea set of scones, finger sandwiches, a selection of desserts and tea for 350,000VND. It's a little hard to find – look for the travel agent, then you'll see a little sign for Rewind Teahouse leading to an alleyway next door, then follow the signs.

11 KEM TRANG TIEN

35 Trang Tien
3772 8080
Open Mon–Sun 8am–10pm
[MAP p. 179 B1]

It's not the most picturesque of spots, but you can't get a more Hanoian ritual than standing around eating ice-cream in this ice-cream parlour housed in an undercover car park. Situated in one of central Hanoi's grandest streets, Kem Trang Tien is an egalitarian kind of place, where everyone can come and buy an ice cream and hang out, either standing, sitting on the back of a motorbike or sitting in the small enclosed street-side cafe. On hot summer nights it's so popular the crowd streams out into the streets, and police have to stop the crowd spilling onto Trang Tien. The decidedly utilitarian, lime green counters sell one or two products each – ice-cream cones on one side, wrapped iced confections on a stick on the other. Flavours range from the traditional – vanilla and chocolate – to the distinctly Vietnamese, such as young green rice.

12 BINH MINH'S JAZZ CLUB

1 Trang Tien
3933 6555
www.minhjazzvietnam.com
Open Mon–Sun 9pm–late
[MAP p. 179 C1]

If the constant Hanoi soundtrack of earsplitting techno is getting to you, come and be soothed by a bit of classy jazz at Binh Minh's Jazz Club. Run by eminent Hanoi musician and teacher Quyen Van Minh, who fell in love with jazz on American and BBC radio in his youth, the club is the centre of Hanoi's jazz scene. Jazz starts at 9pm and the club features open-mic nights and all styles of jazz. If you're lucky, Minh will be playing saxophone with his band. Binh's is situated behind the Hanoi Opera House (*see* p. 26) – find it by walking down the lane between the opera house and Highlands Coffee – in a quiet little bit of Trang Tien.

13 TADIOTO

24B Tong Dan Street
6680 9124
*Open Sun–Wed 8am–11.45pm,
Fri–Sat 8–2am*
[MAP p. 179 C1]

Tadioto (tadiototongdan on
Facebook) is a bit of a hub
in Hanoi's alternative arts
scene – largely due to the
presence of its owner, artist,
journalist and raconteur
Nguyen Qui Duc. Tadioto was
established as an alternative
arts space and bar in 2007
and has since moved around
a bit, its crowd of bohemian
regulars always going with it.
This incarnation of Tadioto is
beautifully decorated in the
rich dark tones so beloved by
the Vietnamese. The bar is
filled with objects that Duc
himself chooses, and includes
some of his artwork. Live jazz
sometimes plays, adding to
the gentle boho ambience.
Its current location is just
near the Hanoi Opera House
(*see* p. 26), around the corner
from Duc's other enterprise,
Japanese noodle bar Moto-San
Uber Noodles, which has great
noodles and banh mi.

HAI BA TRUNG

Hai Ba Trung is an area south of Hoan Kiem Lake and is named after the warrior Trung sisters who, around 40AD, led a rebellion against the Chinese occupation. The district extends from Le Duan, where Hanoi's train station sits, in the west to the Red River in the east. This chapter covers only the northern part of Hai Ba Trung, from Vincom Towers to just below Tran Hung Dao. It's an area that contains the only large central shopping mall, Vincom Towers, and the main Hanoi fabric market, Cho Hom. To the west, you'll find really good street food around Quang Trung and Tran Quoc Toan, as well as the Art Deco houses of Nguyen Gia Thieu. The central area between Pho Hue and Ba Trieu is a lively enclave with a vibrant street life where tangles of phone wires juxtapose against beautiful trees, and where karaoke joints jostle with Japanese restaurants and upmarket apartment buildings – pure Hanoi.

→ *Nguyen Gia Thieu is home to the faded grandeur of many Art Deco houses*

SIGHTS
1. Art Deco Houses

SHOPPING
2. Vincom Towers
3. Cho Hom (Fabric Market)
4. Made in Vietnam

EATING & DRINKING
5. Chim Sao
6. Cong Caphe
7. Bun Cha Huong Lien
8. Café Mai

1 ART DECO HOUSES

Nguyen Gia Thieu
[MAP p. 178 B2]

A neighbourhood full of decaying Art Deco villas, with their flat roofs, curved corners and distinctive gates, lies just north of Thien Quang Lake. Built for wealthy Vietnamese families in the 1930s, the houses are no longer in a good state. However, if you're a fan of the style it's worth taking a short walking tour. Start at the corner of Nguyen Gia Thieu and Lien Tri, the site of the famous 'tipping house', a leaning Art Deco building. Wander up Nguyen Gia Thieu, towards Tran Binh Trong where there are a few villas on either side, some hard to see due to high walls. Turn left at Tran Binh Trong and on the corner of Nguyen Du and Tran Binh Trong, opposite the lake, you'll see two buildings. The grander and most well preserved of the two, 59 Nguyen Du, is now a government guesthouse and worth stopping at for photographs. If you have a tour guide, ask if they can get you inside to see the interior. Otherwise, grab a copy of Linda Mazur's book *Hidden Houses of Hanoi and the Stories They Tell* – which tells the history of these houses.

POCKET TIP

If you're in the area or weekends, check the ca· at Thien Quang Lake to s if the bird club meet-up on – wires will be strung v cages holding birds sing while their owners drink tea.

2 VINCOM TOWER**/**

191 Ba Trieu
3974 9999
www.vincom.com.vn
Open Mon–Sun 9.30am–10pm
[MAP p. 179 A4]

Of use to travellers primarily for its air-conditioning and entertainment options, Vincom's modern twin towers are a startling sight in this area of older low-rise buildings. Nestled on Ba Trieu, Vincom Towers contains retail, entertainment and (surprisingly few) good food and beverage options. Tower One houses a range of Western brands (such as **Maxx**, **Levi's** and **Adidas**), a supermarket and, on the top floor, a cinema showing blockbusters. Tower Two has clothing chains such as Mango and French Connection on the ground floor. The top two floors are dedicated to children's wear and Gamesworld, a dimly-lit floor of games that will keep you entertained for hours. If you want a quiet air-conditioned cafe to hang out in and use the wi-fi, look out for the spacious cafe/co-working space Nest by AIA on the 4th floor, which features beautiful contemporary Scandinavian design.

3 CHO HOM (FABRIC MARKET)

149 Pho Hue
Open Mon–Sun 6am–5pm
[MAP p. 179 A3]

Luxurious wedding-dress fabrics and silks are the stars among the range at Hanoi's main fabric market. It's a little hard find so make sure you have its name and address written in Vietnamese to show people in case you get lost – look for the large 'CHO HOM' sign on Pho Hue. Downstairs the market has food, clothes, jewellery and a wet market. Upstairs is where the fabric stalls are squeezed together in small corridors. It can be a little claustrophobic, so try to remember where you are in relation to the open space of the central light well. Go in the morning when the temperature's cooler; by 11.30am the stallholders break for lunch and a nap. The specialties here are linens, linen/cotton blends and cotton jersey, but the real bargains are the wedding-dress fabrics and silks (around 300,000VND per metre) available at a couple of specialist stalls. Most fabrics are around 70,000 to 100,000VND per metre with more specialist fabrics between 150,000 and 300,000VND. Don't be shy about bargaining hard but little English is spoken so take a calculator (or app).

POCKET TIP
Dong Xuan Market (see p. 6) also has a good selection of fabrics upstairs on the first floor.

4 MADE IN VIETNAM

229 Pho Hue
Open Mon–Sun 9am–9pm
[MAP p. 179 B4]

You never know what brand-name and designer labels you might find when you dig around here. Made in Vietnam is a chain of stores that sell overruns of clothing manufactured in Vietnam; there are shops all around Hanoi, with some specialising in certain labels (these are usually printed on the outside windows) and often with different varieties of stock at different times. Sizing can be tiny (i.e. Asian), but persevere. Not only will there be some Western sizes but also one-off finds of high-end labels. The labels you do often see are Zara, Forever New and North Face, with rare finds including Japan's Earth, Music & Ecology and Seidensticker shirts. Some of the bigger stores (including this one) even have underpants in Western sizes.

HAI BA TRUNG

5 CHIM SAO

65 Ngo Hue
3976 0633
www.chimsao.com
Open Mon–Sun 9am–10.30pm
[MAP p. 179 B3]

Buffalo, eel and frog are all on the menu at this popular restaurant, and it's a good place to start if you'd like to try these more unusual ingredients. A little hidden away in a small building on a side street of boutiques and a beautiful temple off Pho Hue, Chim Sao's dark wood interior combined with high ceilings and vintage Vietnamese furniture gives it a sombre but calm ambience, as preferred by many Vietnamese people. 'Chim' means pigeon, so it's not surprising that a special dish is minced pigeon meat with crispy prawn crackers. The fresh spring rolls are regionally influenced and some are served with unusual ingredients including eggplant and pineapple. They also have a few of the Hanoi standard specialties, such as caramel pork and fried eggplant; mix it up with some of these and a few of the more interesting dishes. Downstairs there are tables with chairs but upstairs seating is on the floor.

6 CONG CAPHE

152D Trieu Viet Vuong
2247 0602
www.congcaphe.com
Open Mon–Sun
7.30am–11.30pm
[MAP p. 179 A4]

This chain of vintage military-themed cafes is part of the new wave of northern Vietnamese nostalgia, a trend that emerged in the last 10 years as Hanoi became more prosperous, and people felt more comfortable looking back to harsher times. This branch was the first Cong Caphe in Hanoi and it's probably the best one. Kitted out with vintage black-and-white family photos, war medals and propaganda posters, (a painted war helmet serves as the lightshade), it's all set against exposed brick, with a cute little mezzanine floor up top. The coffees are just okay and this branch feels more like a bar, so grab a beer and one of the juices and enjoy the trip back in time. It's also worth a visit partly to see this charming neighbourbood, three streets between busy Pho Hue and Ba Trieu just north of Vincom Tower (see p. 41) – Mai Hac De, Trieu Viet Vuong and Bui Thi Xuan – that are full of Japanese restaurants, karaoke bars and apartments.

7 BUN CHA HUONG LIEN

24 Le Van Huu
0904 493322
Open Mon–Sun 10am–7pm
[MAP p. 179 B3]

Even before it gained fame when Anthony Bourdain had lunch here with Barack Obama, Bun Cha Huong Lien was a heavily popular Hanoi institution; the major change is that since the Obama visit the clientele features a lot more foreigners, generally tourists asking where Bourdain and Obama sat. The restaurant is set up like a classic one-dish Hanoi restaurant – cooking station outside at the front, with easy-to-clean metal tables, plastic stools and tiled floors inside. At the back is a stairway that leads to higher floors. As for the bun cha, 85,000VND will get you the 'Obama special' bun cha – noodles, fragrant herbs and smoky pork patties floating in a cold soup-like sauce, a seafood spring roll and a bottle of Hanoi beer. While many other bun cha places are open for just a couple of hours a day, this one is open all day.

8 CAFÉ MAI

96 Le Van Huu
3822 7751
www.cafemai.vn/en
Open Mon–Sun 7am–10pm
[MAP p. 179 B3]

For a taste of old-style Hanoi cafe culture, visit one of the city's great institutions, Café Mai, a family-owned business established in 1936. At Café Mai they roast, grind and serve up delicious Vietnamese-style coffee. Try the café phe sua da (coffee with condensed milk) and discover how the Vietnamese make and take their coffee – teeth-smackingly sweet and strong. Buy some Vietnamese Robusta coffee beans to take away and a little one-cup filter to make your own Vietnamese coffee back home. Try before you buy – the Robusta coffee is quite bitter due to its high caffeine content, which is why Vietnamese people have it with condensed milk.

NHA THO

The area surrounding Nha Tho street is currently the hippest area of Hanoi. It may look a little touristy, but if you know where to go there are some great little spots. Dominated by the large Neo-Gothic cathedral on the corner of Nha Tho and Ly Quoc Su, the area is jam-packed with restaurants, boutiques (with clothes that will fit Westerners), souvenir shops and cafes. The laneways off Ly Quoc Su to the north of Nha Tho are backpacker heaven with a scattering of more upmarket restaurants and some pretty decent street food.

The great sprawling villa at 8 Chan Cam is worth a visit, housing a number of interesting makeshift businesses, and the villa showcases the faded grandeur that makes Hanoi so photogenic. Have a coffee with the locals at one of the many street cafes at the intersection of Ly Quoc Su, Nha Tho and Nha Chung outside St Joseph's Cathedral, or one of the more luxurious establishments on Nha Tho. Nha Tho street itself has some great souvenir shops – basic ones that sell the ubiquitous lacquerware, as well as some upmarket options. South of Nha Tho, Nha Chung has the best souvenir stores as well as some high-end fashion shops. The bia hoi (street beer) stalls opposite the cathedral are famous around Hanoi.

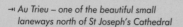

→ *Au Trieu – one of the beautiful small laneways north of St Joseph's Cathedral*

SIGHTS
1. St Joseph's Cathedral

SHOPPING
2. Ipa-Nima
3. Chula
4. Tsnow Boutique
5. Tired City
6. May
7. Collective Memory – the House of Curios
8. Nagu
9. Hanoi Smile

EATING & DRINKING
10. Porte d'Annam
11. Le Petit Bruxelles
12. Pizza 4P's
13. Loading T
14. Van Yen Art Cafe
15. Banh Cuon Ba Hanh
16. Pasteur Street Brewing
17. Mad Botanist – the Gin Specialist

CẤM
ĐỖ Ô TÔ

1 ST JOSEPH'S CATHEDRAL

cnr Nha Chung and Nha Tho
3825 4424
Open Mon–Sun 8am–12pm &
2–6pm
[MAP p. 174 C3]

POCKET TIP
Cua Bac Church also does English-language Catholic mass at 10am on Sunday. You'll find it on 56 Phan Dinh Phung.

Seeing this smaller version of Paris' Notre Dame cathedral in the middle of Hanoi is quite surreal, and a powerful reminder of the years France occupied the country. St Joseph's decaying, romantic beauty is best seen (and photographed) in the late afternoon light, or on some Sundays when the facade is decked out in dramatic flags and religious regalia. Built in 1886 on land formerly belonging to Bao Thien pagoda, which was built under the Ly dynasty, St Joseph's is the headquarters of the Archdiocese of Vietnam. Vietnamese mass is held daily, and there is an English-language mass on Sundays – check signage out the front for times. If you want a closer look at the interior outside of mass times – the elaborate stained glass windows are worth seeing – try the side door. Remember to dress modestly (no shorts) and behave respectfully.

2 IPA-NIMA

5 Nha Tho
3928 7616
www.ipa-nima.com
Open Mon–Sun 9am–8pm
[MAP p. 174 C3]

If you're looking for a handbag in Hanoi, you could go to Hang Dau in the Old Quarter for an imitation designer bag, but why not go for the real deal and visit Ipa-Nima for a more expensive, well-made product, and one that you won't see back home. Plus, you'll have a fun reminder of your holiday to carry around. Ipa-nima has many different kinds of handbags but specialises in glitzier, blingy, limited-edition bags. These are the kind of unabashedly colourful, feminine bags you'd see on the ladies in *Sex and the City*. The Nha Tho showroom is a colourful world of beads, sequins, leather and silk bags and purses, all made in an artisan workshop in Vietnam. To take the sting out of the cost, make sure you keep your receipt for tax back at the airport.

3 CHULA

18 Nha Chung
3710 1102
www.chulafashion.com
Open Mon–Sun 9am–9.30pm
[MAP p. 174 C3]

An unlikely and stylish mix of Spanish and Vietnamese styles, Chula is a not-to-be missed Hanoi institution if you're a fashion lover. Spanish owners Diego Coritzas Del Valle and Laura Fontan Pardo have become fixtures in the Vietnamese fashion scene due to the popularity (both in Vietnam and now internationally) of their very Spanish take on Vietnamese classics like the ao dai (traditional Vietnamese tunic). Using bold Spanish colours and classic Vietnamese images such as mopeds and tangled electricity wires, Chula marries a very Spanish palette of bright, bold colours with Vietnamese silks and images creating wonderfully vibrant statement pieces. Their A-line dresses are a staple and probably the most practical for a traveller. Chula also has a location at 43 Nhat Chieu in Tay Ho, which has a showroom and a bar.

4 T/NOW BOUTIQUE

10A Bao Khanh
0945 236886
Open Mon–Sun 9am–9pm
[MAP p. 174 C2]

If you don't have time to get out to the pottery village of Bat Trang (*see* p. 154), come to this little shop near Hoan Kiem Lake, where you'll find a selection of the best contemporary designs from Bat Trang. The prices here aren't that much higher than at Bat Trang, and the staff are friendly and welcoming and will show you around. If you're a pottery nerd, it's a good way to trend-spot what's happening in the ceramic world and you'll be pleased with the array of glazes, pieces with quirky shapes and textures, serving ware, dinnerware, mugs and plates. The Japanese tea ceremony sets are really popular and the staff are more than happy to individually wrap pieces to safely put in your luggage for you. While you're there, check out the designer fashion shop upstairs selling eclectic minimalist pieces.

NHA THO

5 TIRED CITY

11A Bao Khanh Lane
0462 702900, 0437 100668
www.tiredcity.com
Open Mon–Sun 9am–9pm
[MAP p. 174 C2]

Tired City's founder, Nam, says the shop's name was inspired by his vision of Hanoi as an 'ancient, quiet and melancholic city, with a kind of beauty that makes you want to stop for a while just to contemplate it'. You can see Nam's muted romantic vision of the city in some of his art at Tired City, as well as more energetic designs by Hanoi's hip young artists that feature subverted visions of traditional Viet icons and characters, such as the girl in an ao dai dress or a policeman riding a skateboard. These are featured on notebooks, postcards, posters and t-shirts and make very affordable, compact, not to mention ultracool, souvenirs and gifts. For the more serious art buyer, you can buy prints and pictures on art canvasses. They also stock the best of the retro propaganda posters you'll see round the corner in Ly Quoc Su. The friendly, enthusiastic staff are happy to recommend items and obviously love the shop and their work. They speak great English and are also happy to give recommendations for things to do around Hanoi.

POCKET TIP
There is a second location at 84 Quan Su.

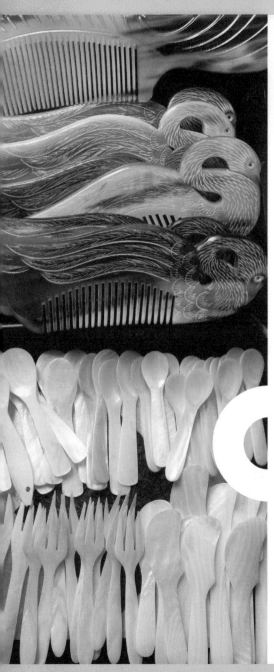

6 MAY

7 Nha Tho
0904 109566
Open Mon–Sun 9am–7pm
[MAP p. 174 C3]

May is a nostalgic, old-fashioned shop that sells simple and elegant pieces, such as little embroidered-cotton lavender or lingerie bags, carefully embroidered tablecloths or simple, refined white cotton handkerchiefs. When you walk into May the first thing you see is a beautifully made up double bed, showcasing their specialty cotton and linen homewares. Behind this, at the back, is a rack of the kind of very useful light, cotton long-sleeved tops that shield against mosquitos. May also stocks jewellery, quilts, buffalo horn trinkets and soft toys.

NHA THO

7 COLLECTIVE MEMORY – THE HOUSE OF CURIOS

20 Nha Chung
0986 474243
www.collectivememory.vn
Open Mon–Sun
9.30am–9.30pm
[MAP p. 174 C3]

Cleverly curated by Hanoi's hippest lifestyle journalist, Nga Hoang, Collective Memory has something for everyone. Of all the places to buy souvenirs and 'curios' in this area, this is the most stylish and original, with many products you won't find anywhere else. Nga regularly travels around Vietnam buying for the shop and has an eye for unusual, often vintage, pieces that won't break the bank – old maps of Hanoi, Indochina-themed bags, Pop Art cushion covers, clothing made from ethnic minority fabrics, pottery, fridge magnets … it really is a house of curios. Nga is often in the shop and happy to chat and give advice on ideas for gifts, or even on cool places to go in Hanoi, so do make sure you say hello!

8 NAGU

20 Nha Tho
3928 8020
www.zantoc.com
Open Mon–Sun 9am–9pm
[MAP p. 174 C3]

Judging by the stylish cream and aqua vintage front door and tiled Nagu sign above, it's obvious that Nagu is a cut above the other gift shops on Nha Tho. Everything in this Japanese-owned gift shop is kawaii (cute), from the Nagu teddy bear, complete with its conical hat (the Nagu signature item, one you'll probably see copied in various other shops around Hanoi), to handmade embroidered purses, handbags and jewellery, as well as homewares such as embroidered linen coasters. The children's clothing collection upstairs is worth a look. While the Made In Vietnam shops (*see* p. 43) have everyday children's wear, these are more bespoke cotton items they can wear for formal occasions.

9 HANOI SMILE

8 Nha Chung, 12 Nha Tho
3828 5681
Open Mon–Sun 10am–7pm
[MAP p. 174 C3]

Lacquerware, bambooware, buffalo-horn goods, handcrafted bags – almost anything you've seen at souvenir shops around Hanoi can be found here. Hanoi Smile is one of many similar shops in the Nha Tho area, stuffed with shelves full of colourful souvenirs, but the staff at both outlets are friendlier and more accommodating than their competitors and they are happy to bargain. It's a cheery, welcoming and slightly overwhelming place – navigating your way in the small space is challenging and the sheer volume of goods would be confusing if they did not keep things immaculately tidy. Silk table runners with the lotus emblem make unusual and luxurious gifts, and there are silk scarves for everyone too. For gifts for kids and super-flexible adults, buy the foot badminton shuttlecocks.

10 PORTE D'ANNAM

22 Nha Tho
3938 2688
www.verticale-hanoi.com
Open Mon–Sun 11am–10pm
[MAP p. 174 C3]

If you're up for a bit of a blowout luxury meal in Hanoi, chances are you'll end up at one of Didier Corlou's restaurants. Corlou is Hanoi's most prolific and longstanding French chef, who specialises in high-end French–Vietnamese fusion cooking. Porte D'Annam, located behind a charming wooden frontage on Nha Tho, is the most accessible of Corlou's ventures, being a kind of bistro rather than a fine-dining establishment. Corlou's love of the spices used in Vietnamese cooking (which you can buy at the little shop downstairs) is evident in all his restaurants and it's expressed in dishes such as the pork ribs with spices and honey, the cheese le Corlou and the desserts. If you've wondered about the much-loved, ubiquitous pomelo – a large green fruit that looks like a grapefruit – try the pomelo salad. The fresh spring roll selection is a must-try. Corlou's other restaurants are also worth visiting – nearby Madame Hien is the place to go for a grand villa experience, and visit La Verticale for his fine dining.

11 LE PETIT BRUXELLE∫

25 Ly Quoc Su
3938 1769
www.le-petit-bruxelles.com
Open Mon–Sun 9am–10pm
[MAP p. 174 C2]

Hanoi has a lot of great French food, most of it high-end, so it's good to find a cosy little down-to-earth Belgian bistro where you can munch on fries and drink Belgian beers such as Kriek, Leffay and Chimay. With a frontage opening onto busy Ly Quoc Su, in summer it's the perfect place to relax with a salad and an ice cold beer in a clean, air conditioned spot and watch the frenetic pace of this busy neighbourhood. Or, in winter, hunker down in a warm cosy room eating classic Belgian dishes like carbonnade, steak tartare, charcuterie plates and even fondue. The staff speak very good English. Look out for their good-value fixed-price lunch menus (149,000VND).

12 PIZZA 4P'S

24 Ly Quoc Su
3622 0500
www.pizza4ps.com
Open Mon–Sun 10am–
10.30pm
[MAP p. 174 C2]

In a city full of surprisingly great pizza restaurants, the rapidly expanding Pizza 4P's chain has emerged as a clear favourite among Hanoians. It was founded by a Japanese entrepreneur, and the Japanese influence has resulted in some unusual toppings, such as the sashimi pizza and okonomiyaki pizza, and the Vietnamese-inspired four-flower pizza. There are also the standard Italian toppings for traditionalists, as well as pasta dishes and really good antipasti put together with quality ingredients. For a real treat, try any dish that uses the house-made burrata, which you can also purchase from the deli counter near the front door. The uncrowded layout with high ceilings is also a new kind of look for Hanoi, the large open space a relief in such a crowded city. Pizza 4P's is a little hard to find, on a laneway off Ly Quoc Su – look for the giant rat street art on the yellow wall.

13 LOADING T

2nd floor, 8 Chan Cam
Open Mon–Sun 8am–6pm
[MAP p. 174 B2]

With the rapid modernisation of Hanoi, the decaying grand French villas, once so prevalent in central Hanoi, are becoming an endangered species. That's why the huge, ramshackle villa at 8 Chan Cam (off Ly Quoc Su) is so special. It's home to a number of businesses – including a clothing boutique, a branch of cutesy floral-craft shop Flora and this sweet indie cafe, set in a large room at the front on the building's first floor. As with so much of old Hanoi, every detail of the interior design – from ornate tiled floor, doric column and exposed brick walls to antique French windows – is gorgeous and, combined with the shabby-chic furnishings, creates a relaxed, bohemian atmosphere. The young staff mostly speak a bit of English and are very friendly. Try the specialty lime coffee or a fruity iced tea or, if you're a fan, the egg coffee.

14 VAN YEN ART CAFE

2E Quang Trung, Hoan Kiem
0963 906969
Open Mon–Sun 7am–11.45pm
[MAP p. 174 C4]

This unpretentious, relaxing cafe is somewhere to watch everyday Hanoians, as they enjoy the little oasis of greenery on the traffic island opposite. Sitting outside on the little plastic stools is the best option, but do pop inside and have a look at the Vietnamese art. During the day you'll find office workers taking a break and relaxing here; at nighttime it's a mixed crowd sipping iced teas and coconut juice from freshly opened coconuts or drinking Hanoi beer from cans. Food options are limited to banh mi with chicken, egg, pâté or smoked ham. It's not a spectacular destination in its own right, but a lovely little spot to have a break with everyday Hanoians if you're nearby.

15 BANH CUON BA HANH

26B Tho Xuong
0961 669626
Open Mon–Fri 6am–10.30pm,
Sat–Sun 7am–10pm
[MAP p. 174 C3]

Banh Cuon Ba Hanh is a cafe and cooking school that specialises in banh cuon – steamed rice paper rolls with fillings such as pork and mushrooms. Sit at a table opposite the open kitchen and watch as chef Ba Hang, an older Vietnamese lady, expertly makes your banh cuon in front of you. The cooking technique seems bizarre at first – thin fabric is stretched over a pot of boiling water, then batter is spread over this fabric and steamed to create a moist, thin and very delicate pancake. The pancake is then carefully removed and rolled up and stuffed with various fillings, then served with nuoc cham dipping sauce. Order one of the sets that include the rice rolls, a drink and one or two other dishes, such as a Vietnamese salad, for 70,000VND or less – note that these are Vietnamese portions (i.e. quite small). If watching Ba Hang make banh cuon isn't enough, you can request a cooking class at the reception of Cinnamon Hotel (walk through the door at the back of the restaurant).

16 PAƧTEUR ƧTREET BREWING

1 Au Trieu
6294 9462
www.pasteurstreet.com
Open Mon–Sun 11am–11pm
[MAP p. 174 B3]

If you've had craft beer in a bar or restaurant in Vietnam, it's likely you've had one of Pasteur Street's brews. They've been brewing in Ho Chi Minh City since 2014, and this is their first Hanoi venture. There's an exposed-brick, distressed-concrete semi-industrial look inside, softened by wooden beams and modern art. The best seat has to be on the terrace overlooking Au Trieu, one of the most charming lanes in this area. The star attraction is a selection of craft beers infused with Vietnamese ingredients. Flavours include Spice Island Saison, infused with lemongrass, ginger and Phu Quoc black pepper; Passionfruit Wheat Ale; Coffee Porter made with Arabica beans from K'Ho Coffee; Pomelo IPA; and Cyclo Imperial Chocolate Stout infused with cacao nibs from Marou Chocolate. The menu tends towards Southern US dishes like Nashville hot chicken, and grilled cheese with soup – great for soaking up a couple of the extra types of beer you might want to try.

17 MAD BOTANIƒT – THE GIN ƒPECIALIƒT

45 Ly Quoc Su
2246 4123
Open Mon–Thurs 9am–
11.45pm, Fri–Sun 9–1am
[MAP p. 174 C3]

This bar calls itself the first
'speakeasy-style gin bar' in
Hanoi, and it certainly lives
up to its name with gorgeous
dark Art Deco interiors and a
choice of more than 100 types
of gin. But the real drawcard
here is the view of St Joseph's
Cathedral (*see* p. 50) from
the 3rd and 4th floors which,
seen after a gin or two from
the roof terrace, looks like
the most romantic thing
ever. Check the Facebook
page (TheMadBotanist) for
events such as salsa nights
and for happy-hour times.
It's set above VPresso, a little
cafe diagonally across from
St Joseph's Cathedral on
Ly Quoc Su, and accessed
via a staircase at the back of
the cafe.

TONG DUY TAN

Close to Hanoi's train station, pedestrianised Tong Duy Tan has long been known as 'food street', a place you can come night or day and get a meal or a drink. It's an area that seems to go in and out of fashion, but right now it's hot, as evidenced by recent openings, including Ne – by Hanoi's superstar bartender Pham Tien Tiep, elegant cafe/artisan shop/ event space Vui Studio, 24-hour cafe/bar/ co-working space Xofa and cute indie paper shop Zo Project. Ngo Cam Chi, which bisects Tong Duy Tan is also worth checking out when you're cruising around for a meal.

When deciding on where to eat it helps if you know a few Vietnamese food terms – the names of the eateries will often be the food they are showcasing. Try snails at Bun Oc Cham, Hanoi-style chicken with rice at Com Dao Ga Rang, or look at the menus with photos and go with the age-old adage of trying a restaurant where you see a lot of locals eating.

→ *Behind the street Tong Duy Tan, houses, shops and cafes sit alongside Hanoi's central railway line*

SHOPPING
1. Zo Project
2. Bo Sua
3. Vui Studio

EATING & DRINKING
4. Xofa Café
5. Hanoi Social Club
6. Ray Quan
7. Ne

1 ZO PROJECT

10A Dien Bien Phu
Open Mon–Fri 10am–7pm,
Sat–Sun 10am–5pm
[MAP p. 177 E3]

Zo Project sells the kind of handmade, original gifts that you might find on Etsy, only this shop is real and in a crazy location, right on Hanoi's main train line. The shop sells traditional Vietnamese 'do' paperware (made from bark). The paper is used to make beautifully decorated and designed products such as notebooks, matchboxes, lanterns, posters and postcards. It's a smart collaboration of the old and young – young artists appreciating the traditional art of paper making and supporting this industry with their own enterprise. The delicate lanterns make wonderful reminders of your trip to Vietnam. The shop is a little hard to find (turn right onto the train track at 5A Tran Phu or 10A Dien Bien Phu, following the rail track to find house no 27), but while you're looking for it, it's fascinating to see how the people on the train line live. Zo Project also runs tours to the paper-making village, where you can get out of Hanoi and see how the Muong ethnic minority who make the paper live, see paper being made and have a go at making and decorating it for yourself.

2 BO SUA

18 Dien Bien Phu
3978 5426
www.bosua.vn
Open Mon–Sun 8am–10pm
[MAP p. 177 E2]

When skateboarder Do Viet
Anh returned to Hanoi in
2001 after living in the Czech
Republic, he found there was
almost no skate scene here
and boards were hard to come
by, so he started importing his
own. This became a business,
Boo Skateshop, and he later
launched Bo Sua, a local youth
streetwear fashion label.
Bo Sua's tongue-in-cheek
designs, riffing on symbols of
Vietnamese life, are printed
on a constantly changing
range of t-shirts (and can be
seen on the skaters practising
in Lenin Square (*see* p. 89),
just up Dien Bien Phu). The
range also extends to other
streetwear clothing and
accessories, all great quality
and usually including larger
sizes. Make sure you get
one of their psychedelic
paper shopping bags, a great
souvenir of Hanoi in itself and
demonstrative of their strong
environmental ethic.

3 VUI ƒTUDIO

3C Tong Duy Tan
0969 841399
Open Mon–Sun 8am–11pm
[MAP p. 177 F3]

Hanoi's recent economic prosperity has brought with it a newly confident and dynamic arts community, brought together by places like Vui Studio, part of the latest trend of hybrid cafe/gallery/shop/working spaces. Step inside and it's like entering another world – cool, quiet, sparse, slow and calm, the complete opposite of the streets outside. Distressed grey walls, natural wood furniture, plenty of light and high ceilings combine to give Vui an ethereal vibe. All the products sold here – including pottery and natural soaps and sprays – have been developed by Vui in conjunction with local makers; their ethos is one of investing in people and helping them bring crafted, authentic products to the public. Downstairs is the cafe and shop, upstairs is an events space for screenings and music concerts (see VUIstudio on Facebook), as well as a co-working space. Workers also have access to a mini-library of art and design books.

4 XOFA CAFÉ

14 Tong Duy Tan
3717 1555
Open 24 hours
[MAP p. 177 E3]

It's quite acceptable to grab a bite to eat then hunker down for a quick nap at Xofa (xofacafe on Facebook), a 24-hour cafe with huge airy rooms filled with comfy sofas (hence the name), set in a large villa about halfway along Tong Duy Tan. The food's not bad either; the extensive offerings include burgers, salads and soups, as well as Vietnamese food, great coffee, juices and alcoholic drinks. Try the passionfruit juice (50,000VND) or a yoghurt from the dessert menu (65,000VND). As it gets later into the morning a new breed of freelance Hanoians appear with laptops, and it becomes a bit of a co-working space. If you like watching live sport, check out Puku next door – very similar, but with more of a sports-bar theme.

POCKET TIP

If you arrive early in the morning at the nearby train station on one of the overnight sleepers, head to Xofa for a snack and a nap.

5 HANOI SOCIAL CLUB

6 Hoi Vu
3938 2117
Open Mon–Sun 8am–11pm
[MAP p. 174 A3]

Run by an Australian living in Hanoi, the Hanoi Social Club is a home away from home for many young expats, frazzled tourists looking for familiarity, and young hip Vietnamese. The cafe sits in a beautiful house on a cute little curved street, a good place to relax, use the wi-fi and have a coffee or a beer. The menu includes Western cafe standards, such as breakfast favourites bircher muesli and avocado toast. Lunch options include quinoa salad and burgers, and there are also some Vietnamese and vegetarian options. There are regular live music nights and other events; details can be found on their Facebook page (TheHanoiSocialClub).

6 RAY QUAN

48 Le Duan, Dong Da
Open Mon–Sun 5pm–late
[MAP p. 177 D3]

Sitting outside Ray Quan when the night train to Sapa thunders past is either going to be a thrilling experience, or take six months off of your life – if you have a nervous disposition, sit inside. Ray Quan could simply trade off its unusual location, literally metres from Hanoi's one railway track, but its great Vietnamese food, bohemian decor and laid-back young crowd make it a place to go for other reasons. The star attractions food-wise are the bar snacks, such as the smoked goose breast and beef jerky; try the mango salad too. The rice wines are popular, but if you're vegetarian stick to the fruit flavours, as some of the others have animal ingredients, such as snake. To find Ray Quan either go to 48 Le Duan and walk south down the railway track or to 8a Nguyen Khuyen and walk north along the tracks.

7 NE

3B Tong Duy Tan
Open Mon–Sun 7pm–2am
[MAP p. 177 F3]

The creation of Hanoi's most famous cocktail – the flamboyant flaming pho cocktail – has to be seen to be believed, and nowhere better than at Ne, a bar owned by the cocktail's creator, Hanoi's superstar mixologist Pham Tien Tiep.

The pho cocktail is flavoured with the pho spices cassia and star anise, and can now be ordered in other bars in Hanoi, but why not try the original version at Ne? If you're lucky Tiep will be there and you'll get to see a master at work. You can also try his other intriguing cocktails infused with different Vietnamese fruit and spices. Look for the neon Ne sign and enter into this sleek, softly lit bar, head down to the comfy armchairs and sofa and settle in for an interesting cocktail or two that you're not going to get back home. Ne sometimes runs cocktail-making classes – check the Facebook page (Nê.Cocktailbar) for details, and also for live music events.

GREATER BA DINH & SURROUNDS

Ba Dinh is a strange mix of civic buildings, parks, monuments and large swathes of suburban areas. To the far west, just off one of central Hanoi's busiest roads, Kim Ma, is an increasingly Korean neighbourhood, and presiding over it all stands the imposing Lotte Tower where, if you're feeling brave and it's a clear day, you can take the elevator to the 65th floor for an incredible view of greater Hanoi. The area surrounding Van Mieu, the Temple of Literature (technically in Dong Da), is a hub of shops, restaurants and cultural activities. To the north of this are many of Hanoi's biggest tourist attractions – including the Vietnam Military History Museum and the Ho Chi Minh Mausoleum and Museum. While in the area have a wander and check out the impressive mustard yellow government buildings surrounding Ba Dinh Square, then walk around the streets off Dien Bien Phu where some of the grand embassies lie. In the early evening, especially on the weekends, Lenin Square transforms from an empty, lifeless park to a place to meet up, exercise, drink tea, skateboard and hire children's electric cars.

→ *Hanoi's most popular tourist attraction for both foreigners and Vietnamese is the Ho Chi Minh Mausoleum*

CHỦ TỊCH
HÔ · CHÍ · MINH

SIGHTS
1. Vietnam Fine Arts Museum
2. Goethe Institut
3. Temple of Literature (Van Mieu)
4. Ho Chi Minh Mausoleum & Museum
5. Vietnam Military History Museum
6. Lenin Square

SHOPPING
7. Craft Link
8. Indigo Store

EATING & DRINKING
9. KOTO
10. Café CCCP

1 VIETNAM FINE ARTS MUSEUM

66 Nguyen Thai Hoc
3823 3084
www.vnfam.vn
Open Mon–Sun 8.30am–5pm
[MAP p. 176 B2]

Not only is Vietnam Fine Arts Museum somewhere to admire art, it's a place to learn about the fascinating history of the country, as depicted by the country's artists over the years. Housed in a pair of grand French colonial–era buildings, set at the back of a serene garden off one of Hanoi's main thoroughfares, the museum is a calm, peaceful (and air-conditioned) place to view the country's best fine art. The collection covers different historic periods; the French influence during colonisation is particularly evident, though there's little explanation provided. Indian and Khmer influences are evident in the intricately carved Cham-era stone sculptures, reminders of the amazing Cham empire that ruled parts of Vietnam and Cambodia between 2 and 15AD. It's worth reading up on Cham history to get the most out of what you see here. The gift shop is worth seeking out for the art prints. Tickets cost 40,000VND and you'll need to leave your belongings in a locker at the entry point.

2 GOETHE INSTITUT

56–58 Nguyen Thai Hoc
3734 2251
www.goethe.de
Open Mon–Sun 9am–7pm
[MAP p. 176 B2]

Part of Hanoi's charm is its beautiful hidden courtyards and the Goethe's is one of the best. It's bright and modern, with a large green wall at one end and hanging pot plants and colourful flowers everywhere. Part of the charm is its setting, housed between the black and white Art Deco buildings of the Goethe Institut, a cultural institute that promotes the German language and cultural exchanges with Germany around the world. The institute is a busy, vibrant place, that houses offices, classrooms, a library, exhibition spaces and a cafe. The doner kebab seller (it's a surprisingly popular food in Hanoi) out front of the Goethe is a permanent fixture and many prefer these offerings to the meals in the cafe, where there are Vietnamese and German staples. Details of Goethe Institut's events, such as film festivals, documentary-making courses and art exhibitions, can be found on its website.

3 TEMPLE OF LITERATURE (VAN MIEU)

Quoc Tu Giam St, Dong Da
3845 2917
Open Tues–Sun 8am–5.30pm
[MAP p. 176 A2]

Watching nervous students rubbing the heads of statues, hoping for good luck in their upcoming exams, is one of those moments where all cultural differences seem to melt away. We've all been there. The Temple of Literature was Hanoi's first university, built on the orders of Emperor Ly Thanh Thong, and is now a Confucian temple dedicated to literature and learning in the centre of Hanoi. Chinese design elements that were influential in Vietnam at the time of construction in 1070 dominate, such as the outer wall and five courtyards. Its main feature is the third courtyard, featuring a pond and well and 82 stone tortoise statues with the names of the university's doctoral graduates engraved on a slab on their backs – this is where the students come for luck. There's not a lot of signage throughout the temple, but you can buy an English information booklet at the ticket office (8000VND) or hire an English-speaking guide – ask at the ticket office for a referral.

4 HO CHI MINH MAUSOLEUM & MUSEUM

Hung Vuong, Dien Bien
3845 5128
www.bqllang.gov.vn
Opening times vary;
check website
[MAP p. 180 A3, B2]

Situated on the spot where Ho Chi Minh proclaimed Vietnam's independence in 1945, is the Ho Chi Minh Mausoleum, which contains his embalmed body. Built at the meeting point of what were three of Hanoi's grandest boulevards, it is one of the city's most striking buildings. The queue to get in can be very long (up to two or three hours) so take some water, snacks and a hat, and get to know the locals who come from all over Vietnam to pay their respects to the most revered person in Vietnam's recent history, Ho Chi Minh. Once you're inside the mausoleum, the line moves quickly and you will only have a minute or so to view Ho Chi Minh's embalmed body. Etiquette is very strict here (even, quite unusually, for children) so make sure you behave in a respectful manner – cover up, don't take photos inside or fold your arms, and follow the directions of the guards.

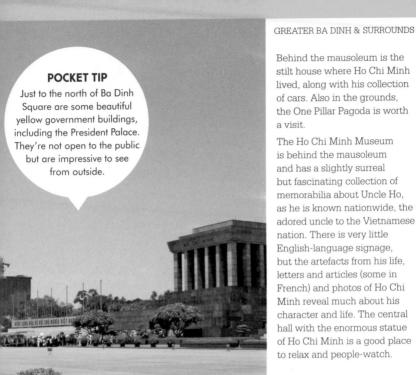

POCKET TIP

Just to the north of Ba Dinh Square are some beautiful yellow government buildings, including the President Palace. They're not open to the public but are impressive to see from outside.

Behind the mausoleum is the stilt house where Ho Chi Minh lived, along with his collection of cars. Also in the grounds, the One Pillar Pagoda is worth a visit.

The Ho Chi Minh Museum is behind the mausoleum and has a slightly surreal but fascinating collection of memorabilia about Uncle Ho, as he is known nationwide, the adored uncle to the Vietnamese nation. There is very little English-language signage, but the artefacts from his life, letters and articles (some in French) and photos of Ho Chi Minh reveal much about his character and life. The central hall with the enormous statue of Ho Chi Minh is a good place to relax and people-watch.

5 VIETNAM MILITARY HISTORY MUSEUM

28A Dien Bien Phu
3823 4264
www.btlsqsvn.org.vn
Open Tues–Thurs & Sat–Sun
8–11.30am & 2–4pm
[MAP p. 177 D1]

Visitors to Hanoi are often surprised at how little evidence there is of the Vietnam War (or the American War, as it is known in Vietnam) in the streets of Hanoi. But some impressive evidence of the country's fights for independence can be seen here – from their battles against the Chinese to the French and the Americans, all invaders they fought and defeated. The museum has photos and artefacts but little explanation in English to put them in context. The model recreation of the Battle of Dien Bien Phu, with a soundtrack of sound effects and original film footage, is worth seeing; otherwise marvel at the military hardware on display outside; some of the most impressive pieces are around the back. Also worth a visit is the Flag Tower, built in 1812, officially part of the citadel next door. As well as the entry fee, you will have to pay a fee to take photos. The museum is not air-conditioned and can be very hot, so an early-morning visit is recommended in summer.

6 LENIN SQUARE

28A Dien Bien Phu
[MAP p. 176 C1]

Hanoians really know how to use their open spaces, though it's only after hours that these spots really come alive. Visit Lenin Square in the middle of the day, and it's just a big empty square with a huge statue of Lenin and some large trees, but if you get up early (around 6am), the park is filled with elderly Vietnamese doing ballroom dancing, samba, meditation or just catching up at a tea stall, perched on tiny little chairs. In the early evening, particularly on weekends, the area in front of the Lenin statue becomes a crazy playground for kids, with children on pedal cars and scooters whirling around in joyful mayhem, sullen teenage skaters and rollerbladers doing jumps down the steps, and older Hanoians doing their daily exercises and socialising. This square, known as Lenin Square due to the large statue of Lenin towering over it, is opposite the Vietnam Military History Museum (*see* p. 88).

POCKET TIP
There are two public spaces named in Lenin's honour in Hanoi – the other one is called Lenin Park and is in Hai Ba Trung district

V.I. LÊ-NIN

7 CRAFT LINK

43-51 Van Mieu, Dong Da
3733 6101
www.craftlink.com.vn
Open Mon–Sun 9am–6pm
[MAP p. 176 A4]

Shopping at one of Hanoi's many social enterprise or fair trade businesses means you get products that are worth buying as much for their quality design and production as the warm fuzzy feeling you get when making a purchase. One of the best is Craft Link, a fairtrade, not-for-profit organisation that promotes work by local artisans, and encourages the preservation and revival of traditional Kinh and ethnic-minority cultures through handicraft production. All the communities they work with must pay fair wages, keep workers safe and be environmentally responsible. There are two Craft Link shops on Van Mieu; this one sells mostly handicrafts, and another shop further up Van Mieu sells jewellery, homewares and trinkets. Make sure you visit the hidden room up on the first floor – walk through the first room you come to, then head out onto the balcony and into the next room. The products in here are more upmarket – mother of pearl handbags, clutches and beautiful clothing.

8 INDIGO ꟷTORE

33A Van Mieu, Dong Da
3719 3090
Open Mon–Sun 8am–7pm
[MAP p. 176 B3]

If you're sick of traipsing around museums or hanging out in cafes, an indigo dyeing workshop is a pretty relaxing and informative way to spend a couple of hours. Dyeing fabric with indigo is still practiced by some ethnic groups in Vietnam, and this place offers the opportunity not just to buy fabrics, but to dye them yourself. Founded by a Vietnamese/ Japanese couple, the Indigo Store also sells handmade Japanese-influenced clothing and other textile-based products such as cushions and scarves, predominantly using indigo and other traditional, natural dyes on handwoven cotton and hemp. Some of the fabrics are printed using shibori and tie-dyed techniques and these can be learned in the two-hour dyeing workshop. Teacher Ms Tho is a friendly, highly skilled textile worker who loves to share her knowledge and you get to take home the fabric you have dyed. Make sure you look at the traditional clothing collection too as they have some very special and rare pieces on display.

9 KOTO

59 Van Mieu, Dong Da
3747 0337
www.koto.com.au
Open Mon–Sun 7.30am–10pm
[MAP p. 176 A4]

KOTO stands for Know One
Teach One, an apt name
for a social enterprise that
trains disadvantaged youth
in hospitality and life skills.
More than 600 of its graduates
have now been employed
and many return to teach.
Originally started in 1999 as a
sandwich bar by Jimmy Pham
with the help of Australian
chef Tracey Lister, KOTO now
occupies two premises on Van
Mieu opposite the Temple of
Literature (see p. 84). One is
a smaller restaurant serving
street-food dishes during
the day, while its flagship
restaurant next door, with a
bar as well as more formal
dining, is extremely popular
with tourists for lunch and
dinner. The food is good, as
are the drinks, but what really
makes it special are the very
sweet, enthusiastic staff who
clearly relish practicing their
English and learning new skills.
The menu is extensive and
has a good mix of Vietnamese
and English dishes, and your
support of this enterprise helps
finance the training program.
There's also a small shop
selling KOTO merchandise.

10 CAFÉ CCCP

103 Ngo 84, Giang Vo
3835 2065
Open Mon–Sun 10am–11pm
[MAP p. 172 C3]

Eating stodgy Ukranian food in a non-descript part of Hanoi is probably not what you were planning for your holiday to the city, however if you a) have a passion for either Ukranian food or culture or b) have seen the classic Hanoi sights and want to do something a bit unusual, then Café CCCP might be for you. Café CCCP comes from a time when a more hardline Communist Vietnam and the Eastern bloc were closely aligned and, judging by the décor, it really hasn't changed much since then. Café CCCP is a Ukranian/Russian restaurant selling comfort food such as borscht, rissoles and blinis. Run by a Vietnamese/Ukranian family, the restaurant is like a Ukranian living room from 30 years ago, complete with resident cat and dog, with dark wooden tables and benches topped with checked tablecloths. There are Russian advertising posters on the wall and Ukranian pop-music videos play on the television. Order a vodka and pickle to start, some Ukranian beers, a plate of the homemade black bread, fried potatoes, pelmeni dumplings with sour cream then finish off with the dessert blintz.

BA DINH – TRUC BACH

Between the Old Quarter and Tay Ho, Truc Bach (pronounced chuc bac) is a neighbourhood known in Hanoi for its bohemian residents and for being the birthplace of pho cuon (steamed stuffed rice noodle rolls), one of the city's most beloved street foods.

The attraction of Truc Bach Lake is less about the lake itself, which has rubbish strewn around its banks, however the parks, local cafes and bars, and charming neighbourhoods near the lake are a great reason to wander about this area. On the south side there are beautiful parks where you'll see Hanoians doing early-morning and evening exercise, and overlooking these are cafes where you can have a cup of tea or try the local brew, Truc Bach beer. Rent a pedal swan boat and go cruising on the lake, or have a meal with locals at the bia hoi (street beer) stall next door. Across the lake is Chau Long market, one of the last wet markets in central Hanoi, and jutting into the lake next to this is the picturesque neighbourhood, Ngu Xa, where you can get some stunning photographs of the gorgeous little streets. This is where the dish pho cuon (rice paper rolls) was born, and every restaurant owner will tell you they invented it. The causeway that divides Truc Bach from Tay Ho also has lakeside parks on its north side and a popular ice-cream cafe.

→ *Early morning at Long Bien market where green mangoes, lychees, mangosteens and rambutans are piled high*

1 TRAN QUOC PAGODA

Thanh Nien
Open Mon–Sun 7.30–11.30am
& 1.30–6.30pm
[MAP p. 183 D3]

Tran Quoc Pagoda, the oldest Buddhist temple in Hanoi, was built in the 6th century. It is perched on a small island jutting out into Ho Tay Lake (*see* p. 134), just off Thanh Nien causeway (which separates Truc Bach Lake from Ho Tay Lake). A front courtyard houses colourful stupas and a tower, and to the right is the altar room. Monks live in the pagoda and can be seen moving about the complex. Be sure to cover knees and shoulders and be respectful of worshippers when taking photos. Look out for the beautiful Bodhi tree, a gift from visiting Indian president Rajendra Prasad in 1959, which is supposed to have been taken as a cutting from the original tree where the Buddha sat and achieved enlightenment.

2 MOSAIC TILED WALL

Nghi Tam, Yen Phu and
Tran Quang Khai
www.hanoimural.blogspot.
com.au
[MAP p.183 E2]

If you're travelling between the Old Quarter and Tay Ho, you'll probably go along the 'dyke road' – the busy, chaotic road that keeps much of Hanoi safe from Red River flooding. Along a 4km (2.5mi) section of this road, on the river side, look out for the mosaic tiled wall, a piece of public art and the longest tiled wall in the world. The wall was the brainchild of arts journalist Nguyen Thu, and was approved and funded by the government as an event to celebrate Hanoi's 1000th birthday in 2010. It provides an entertaining distraction if you're ever stuck in traffic – see if you can spot the turtle with the sword in its mouth, one of Hanoi's most-loved icons. The wall features small murals designed and constructed by international and Vietnamese artists (many from Bat Trang village), with themes from Vietnamese history. At the intersection of Yen Phu and Nghi Tam, next to An Duong gate, you'll see stylised images from the bronze-age Dong Son era in Vietnam (from 1000BC to 1AD) depicting boats, pelican, fish and traditional houses.

97

3 54 TRADITION∫

30 Hang Bun
3715 1569
www.54traditions.vn
Open Mon–Sun 8am–6pm
[MAP p. 181 A2]

Walk into the dark, front room of 54 Traditions, and it's so packed with ancient treasures you'll almost believe you're in a kids adventure movie, about to discover a magical amulet. Each carefully selected piece in this incredible museum/shop has a story to tell, and it's pretty easy to let your imagination go wild – particularly in the shamanic room, which contains religious robes and ceremonial artefacts used in rituals.

Owner Nhung or one of her knowledgeable staff will take you on a tour of the five floors of artefacts, textiles and art from the 54 ethnic groups around the country. It's easy to forget you're in a shop, as the work is presented as if it's in a museum, and the easy-going staff are more like tour guides, with little pressure to buy. The history and craftsmanship on display is incredible, and many international museums purchase from this collection. While 54 Traditions caters for serious collectors of ethnic minority art, it also has prints and knickknacks, and is worth a visit for that special piece you might want to splurge on.

4 DUYEN'S LONG BIEN MARKET TOUR

01687 941737
www.chefduyen.com
Tours Mon–Sun 5.30am
[MAP p. 181 B2]

The vibrant tropical fruit and vegetables sold at Long Bien Market are a photographer's dream; the textures and colours of Asia are all here. This is Hanoi's central wholesale market, supplying fresh produce to the city's restaurants and hotels. The market is also a particularly chaotic, busy and confusing place, which is why it's a good idea to take this tour with Chef Duyen, a Hanoi chef who knows the vendors, the produce and how to cook it better than anyone. Duyen is an experienced and watchful guide, gently pulling a photographer out of the way of a passing motorbike without missing a beat of her explanations of various produce, negotiating with a tofu-making family to let her clients photograph them at work, and translating queries. The tour begins at around 5:30am, just before the vendors pack up, and costs around 1,250,000VND. Afterwards Duyen will take you to sample some local dishes and to one of her favourite noodle joints for a well-earned breakfast and coffee. She also gives tours of the spice section of Dong Xuan market.

99

5 HANOI COOKING CENTRE

44 Chau Long
3715 0088
www.hanoicookingcentre.com
Open Mon–Sun
8.30am–5.30pm
[MAP p. 183 E4]

If you love Vietnamese food, this is the place to learn how to make it yourself. Hanoi Cooking Centre was started by Australian chef Tracey Lister, author of four Vietnamese cookbooks and a longtime resident of Hanoi. Tracey has since moved back to Australia but the cooking classes and street food tours she designed are still run by the staff she trained, many coming from social enterprise training restaurant KOTO (*see* p. 92). The centre has a quiet cafe, with a roof terrace as well as a peaceful courtyard. The cafe serves Western and Vietnamese food. Grab a book from Bookworm (*see* p. 102) next door and settle in with some spring rolls or the addictive pita bread with dips. If you're a real foodie, try one of the Chau Long Market tours followed by a cooking class; it's a great way to learn about the cuisine and culture. The street-food tour is also a good way to sample many great dishes, at locations that typify the best of Vietnamese dishes.

POCKET TIP
HCC founder Tracey Lister regularly comes back to Vietnam to run culinary tours to Hanoi, Halong Bay and Hue, see traceylister.com for information

6 CHAU LONG MARKET

Chau Long
Open Mon–Sun 6.30–11.30am
& 2.30–5.30pm
[MAP p. 183 E4]

Wet markets across Asia are fast disappearing to make way for supermarkets, which makes the working food market of Chau Long that bit more special. If you're a fan of Vietnamese cooking, it's exciting to see very fresh, authentic versions of the ingredients that can be hard to find in the West, as well as many you've never seen before. You will need to have a strong stomach for some of the things you see here – frogs being killed and skinned whole, animals so freshly slaughtered they're still warm, and blood on benches and walls. It's a visceral, raw market experience – noisy, smelly and slightly confusing – but if you are a cook or just a foodie, it's endlessly interesting and all very photogenic. If you're around between 10.30am and 11am you may witness a strange phenomenon – stallholders putting on music and doing their exercises in their stalls.

7 BOOKWORM

44 Chau Long
3715 3711
www.bookwormhanoi.com
Open Mon–Sun 9am–7pm
[MAP p. 183 E4]

Hanoi maps, Hanoi-themed activity books for kids and even a Hanoi version of the Monopoly board game can all be found at Bookworm, one of the few English-language bookshops in Hanoi and by far the most comprehensive. Located behind the Hanoi Cooking Centre (*see* p. 100), next to a lovely courtyard, Bookworm has welcoming well-read English-speaking staff, including knowledgable owner Truong. It's known around Hanoi as the place to buy novels, guidebooks (look out for Nancy Chandler's illustrated map of Hanoi) and children's books, as well as having one of the best collections of English-language books on Vietnamese history located upstairs. If you're looking for particular books, the Facebook page (BookwormHanoi) shows second-hand books that have recently come in.

POCKET TIP
Great imported French cheese is surprisingly easy to find in Hanoi; it's worth ordering the cheese plate.

8 A LA FOLIE

11B Truc Bach
3976 1667
Open Mon–Sun 11am–10pm
[MAP p. 183 D2]

French bistro and bar
A la folie has plenty of 'bonnes vibrations' or good vibes, due to the very relaxed, happy French expats that call the place home. Have a drink at the bar downstairs and do a bit of people-watching along this busy strip, hang out in an armchair with a glass of wine and some charcuterie on the second floor in the lounge/cafe, or have a meal with a romantic view of the lake in the third-floor restaurant. Food-wise, it has everything you'd expect from a good French bistro – standards such as fish soup, soufflé, chicken with merguez (North African sausage) and couscous or steak. It's not cheap, but the fixed-price menu is always good value.

9 STATE-RUN FOOD SHOP NO 37 (MAU DICH)

37 Nam Trang
3715 4336
Open Mon–Sun 10am–10pm
[MAP p. 183 E3]

Harking back to the post-war Bao Cap era, when food was rationed and exchanged for coupons, the concept and decor at this restaurant takes you back to a time of economic and political hardship for communist Vietnam. Old reel-to-reel tape recorders and other museum pieces adorn the walls, but the excellent home-style Hanoi cooking is the real attraction here. The dish I always order is the com chay (white rice crisped up in the bottom of a pot). Also good are the Hanoi spring rolls, fried tofu and the morning glory with garlic. It's a little hard to find this restaurant, which is located on the little peninsula called Ngu Xa that juts out into Truc Bach Lake, but it's really worth it. After your meal make sure you have a wander around the peninsula, one of the most photogenic, quiet and peaceful neighbourhoods in central Hanoi, full of old houses, elderly folk sitting on the streets, children playing and views of Truc Bach Lake.

10 PHO HUYEN

31 Chau Long
0912 769129
Open Mon–Sun 7am–9.30pm
[MAP p. 183 E4]

The pho at this small restaurant is quite different to anything you find in the West. It's the real deal – a surprisingly light, fragrant broth where the flavour intensifies with each mouthful – and may well be the best pho ga (chicken pho) in Hanoi. If it's a nice day, sit outside next to the mural of Venice among the lush plants and birds singing in their cages, and watch locals heading back from Chau Long market (*see* p. 101) with their produce, or the parking attendants gossiping in the street. Make sure you order the quay – fried dough sticks that you can either rip up or dip into the soup – it certainly detracts from the healthiness of the dish but is a wonderful accompaniment! Not much English is spoken and there's no menu, but you're only going there for one thing, so pointing and smiling will get you what you need. You'll find Pho Huyen opposite the Hanoi Cooking Centre (*see* p. 100).

11 BUN CHA HANG THAN

34 Hang Than
3927 0879
Open Mon–Sun 7am–5pm
[MAP p. 181 A2]

For many people, a visit to Hanoi is the first time they've tried bun cha and to most it's a revelation – smoky charcoal-grilled pork served in a kind of cold soupy sauce with noodles, fresh herbs and lettuce. Bun Cha Hang Than is an institution, which means that (unlike the less established street-food stalls in Hanoi) it will probably still be there when this book is published and open when you want to go there. Outside the restaurant sit all the elements of bun cha ready to be assembled – huge baskets of thin white rice noodles, tubs of glistening fresh greens and a wonderfully aromatic barbecue churning out lightly charred little pork patties and rashers of pork. The simple menu is taped to the wall with prices – 'Bun cha 35,000, nem 10,000' (nem are the Hanoi version of fried spring rolls, filled with a pork and mushroom mixture). Sit and slurp up all the yumminess to feel like a local. Be warned, portions are small, so you may need two serves to get your fix of this highly addictive dish.

12 1946

3 Ngo Yen Thanh, off 61
Cua Bac
0909 661946
www.1946.vn
Open Mon–Sun 9am–10pm
[MAP p. 183 E4]

A doorman in a 1940s military uniform signals the vintage '40s theme of this restaurant. Locals and some foreigners come for the retro feel and specialty dishes you won't get at many other restaurants in Hanoi, with dishes such as dragon fish, whole fried baby shrimp and rice-paddy crabs with betel leaves. Start the meal with the pickled cabbage and green mango and a local Truc Bach beer, then order a few dishes to share. Although it's a restaurant, customers treat it like a bia hoi (street beer stall) so don't be surprised to see rubbish thrown on the floor as you do at more informal local places, and only occasionally swept up by staff. Downstairs seating is tables and chairs, or venture upstairs if you don't mind floor seating. The rice wine here is good quality and house-made, so enjoy it (with caution!). It's a little hard to find – look for the neon 1946 sign in an alleyway off Cua Bac.

13 PHO CUON HUNG BEN

35 Nguyen Khac Hieu
3829 2040
Open Mon–Sun 7am–10pm
[MAP p. 183 E3]

Many Hanoians come out here to Ngu Xa, the peninsula that juts into Truc Bach Lake, just to eat pho cuon, steamed rolled rice noodles. Pho Cuon Hung Ben does a pretty good version of the dish, but for a dish you won't get in many other places, try the pho chien phuong (55,000VND), chunks of rice-noodle dough deep fried into little pillows, crispy on the outside and chewy on the inside, topped with stir-fried beef and vegetables in a delicious gravy, and perfect with a beer. Sit inside the small, airless dining room with local families, or join the throngs waiting outside for takeaway and eat it at your hotel. Staff have limited English but there is an English version of the menu you can point at. Also try their fried beef noodles (55,000VND) and sweet potato chips (35,000VND).

108

14 MANZI

14 Phan Huy Ich
3716 3397
Open Mon–Sun 9–12am
[MAP p. 181 A2]

If you're into modern art and want to check out what's happening in Vietnam, Manzi is the place to go. At first glance it seems like every other gorgeous Hanoi cafe-bar cliche – a beautifully restored French-style villa, with shuttered windows and large airy rooms – but venture upstairs and you'll find one of Hanoi's most cutting-edge art galleries. You can buy some of the art – ask the knowledgeable English-speaking staff for information on Vietnamese artists featured. When the weather is fine, head outside to the terrace. The cafe's menu selection is very limited, but the attraction here is the art and the beautiful building, so have a wander with a cup of tea and enjoy a visual feast. Manzi often has music and art events so check out the Facebook page (manzihanoi) for information on when things are on.

15 STANDING BAR

170 Tran Vu
3266 8057
www.standingbarhanoi.com
Open Tues–Sat 4pm–12am,
Sun 2.30pm–12am
[MAP p. 183 E3]

Set in a beautiful old house in a lovely quiet neighbourhood overlooking Truc Bach Lake, about 20 minutes' walk from the Old Quarter, the Standing Bar is the perfect place to get away from the craziness of Hanoi, have a craft beer and enjoy the sunset. This bar is known for its large range of craft beers and ciders from around Vietnam – 19 and growing in the taproom – and the perfect beer snack, yakitori skewers. Other food choices include small plates of Vietnamese bar snacks and tapas, as well as standard bar snacks like chips. Standing Bar also has regular comedy nights as well as live music acts and other events in English – see the Facebook page (standingbarhanoi) to find out what's on.

TAY HO – QUANG AN

The most gentrified, and most peaceful, part of the already upmarket neighbourhood of Tay Ho is Quang An – a large piece of land protruding into West Lake, where rich Vietnamese and foreigners alike raise families and patronise the upmarket shops, restaurants and spas. Once an area filled with cumquat trees and small lakes, today Quang An is populated by massive French-style villas, and increasingly, large luxury apartment complexes. The main street, To Ngoc Van, is filled with shops and restaurants and is the hub of the expat community. Just around the corner, busy Xuan Dieu has some good shops and cafes, as well as the area's small shopping mall Syrena Shopping Centre. It's worth having a walk through the back lanes north of To Ngoc Van to see the grand villas. On Sunday mornings locals ride bikes around the lake, stopping in various parks for tea breaks of super-caffeinated green tea and coffee. It's worth a wander up past Hanoi Rock City and O'Douceurs patisserie to see the incredible gymnastics of the game of foot badminton on the shores of Quang Ba Lake. It's also where, if you're there between June and August, you'll see fields of lotus flowers, Hanoi's favourite flower.

→ *Lakeside pagoda Phu Tay Ho sits on a quiet street that's lined with fortune tellers and shops*

SIGHTS
1. Phu Tay Ho

SHOPPING
2. Module 7
3. Clom's Closet
4. Copenhagen Delights
5. L'atelier
6. Fivimart
7. Emporium
8. Future Traditions

EATING & DRINKING
9. Joma Café
10. Gelato Italia
11. Zenith Yoga Studio and Cafe
12. Bia Hoi Nha Hang 68
13. Furbrew
14. Don's Bistro
15. Hanoi Rock City

1 PHU TAY HO

Thanh Nien & Co Ngu
Open Mon–Sun 7.30–11.30am
& 1.30–6.30pm
[MAP p. 184 A2]

If you're going to do just one cultural thing in Hanoi, visit a lakeside temple or pagoda. Witnessing locals performing temple rituals in beautiful, peaceful surrounds is strangely touching. Phu Tay Ho is my favourite temple, nestled in an area that feels like a little rural village. On the road leading to the temple, stalls sell one of Hanoi's specialty dishes, banh tom (sweet potato and prawn fritters) as well as offerings for altars in the temple – boxes of biscuits, fruit and flowers. The temple sits in a peaceful spot on the edge of Ho Tay Lake (*see* p. 134) and is dedicated to the mother goddess Princess Lieu Hanh, daughter of the Jade Emperor, who was sent to help farmers, blessing them with good crops. After entering the ornate gates, you will see a courtyard to the right, featuring statues of buffaloes. Turn left and you will arrive at the main temple. Inside, you will see three goddess statues with their male servants, and animals that represent animist beliefs. The goddesses are Mau Thuong Ngan, who wears green and represents the forests; Mau Thoai, who wears white and represents water; and Mau Dia, who wears gold, representing the earth.

POCKET TIP

On special days in the lunar month, fortune tellers and calligraphers line the street to the temple.

114

2 MODULE 7

83 Xuan Dieu
3719 7247
www.module7design.com
Open Mon–Sun 9am–7pm
[MAP p. 185 A2]

The dramatic bamboo entrance at Module 7, an interior-design agency and furnishing shop catering to expats and rich Vietnamese, gives you an idea of the high level of design and craftsmanship in the store's wares. The collection here is beautifully curated – every item is handpicked, elegant and original. The stylish furniture, textiles, clothing and pottery are made using local materials and proudly showcase Vietnamese contemporary design. Check out the range of lampshades crafted from repurposed traditional items such as fish nets and conical hats, and the modern take on lacquerware in the form of brightly coloured jewellery boxes, sleek black chests of drawers and a Cubist-inspired set of multicoloured tables. If something here really takes your fancy, talk to staff about packing and shipping it back for you.

3 CLOM'S CLOSET

31 Xuan Dieu
3718 8233
www.clomscloset.com
Open Mon–Sun 9am–7pm
[MAP p. 185 B3]

It's surprisingly hard to find reliable, skilled tailors in Hanoi, particularly ones who can work quickly. Clom's Closet can do a turnaround of two to three days, so you can put in an order, head off for that Halong Bay (*see* p. 150) or Sapa (*see* p. 158) trip, and your clothes will be ready when you get back. Owner Mizuki say Clom's individual approach is like having a personal stylist – they try to make clothes that suit your lifestyle, tastes and body shape. This focus, together with strong attention to detail, results in durable, wearable, one-of-a-kind, simple clothes, often with a very Japanese aesthetic. The huge range of fabrics you see artfully hung over a huge bamboo frame in the front room are all imported, mostly neutral, cotton fabrics that are perfect for Hanoi's heat. You can buy ready-made outfits such as shirt dresses, the kind of thing you can wear day to night with different accessories and loose-fitting blouses to pair with jeans. Check out their Instagram (@clomscloset).

4 COPENHAGEN DELIGHTS

55 Xuan Dieu
3718 4395
www.copenhagendelights.com
Open Mon–Sun 8.30am–5pm
[MAP p. 185 B2]

In the days of throwaway generic cheap and cheerful kids clothes, it's a relief to find a shop like Copenhagen Delights. The clothes here are beautiful – classic children's clothes with a northern European sensibility that you would pay a lot more for elsewhere – including gorgeous sashed party frocks and collared dress shirts. The matching mother-and-daughter dresses are beyond cute. The clothes are high quality, made from strong cottons, bamboo fabrics and denims, and are well made so they last and last. And if you've forgotten swimming costumes for the kids, it's one of the only places in Hanoi where you'll find quality kids swimsuits and sunsuits. They also sell a few accessories such as little melamine trinkets and modern takes on lacquerware.

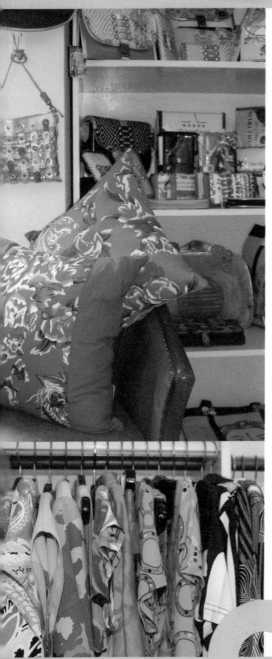

5 L'ATELIER

33 Xuan Dieu
3718 6758
www.ateliervietnam.com
Open Mon–Sun 9am–8pm
[MAP p. 185 B3]

Using beautiful fabrics and the rich colour palette of Vietnam, Duyen Huong produces high-quality designer clothes. You can see a French influence in her elegant and chic designs complemented by the accessories she stocks for her clients, like the unique fusion of French style and Vietnamese materials and craftsmanship of Valerie Cordier's range of bags. Come here for Western-size shoes, loose shift dresses and chunky accessories. Make sure you check out the back room, with a range of beautiful souvenirs: tea towels printed with photos of old Hanoi, note books, and cushion covers featuring the ubiquitous red floral fabric found throughout Vietnam and China, as well as myriad silk products.

6 FIVIMART

1st floor, Syrena Shopping
Centre, Xuan Dieu
Open Mon–Sun 8am–9.30pm
[MAP p. 185 B2]

The Fivimart chain of
supermarkets are the nearest
you'll get to a Western-style
supermarket in central Hanoi.
Situated up the escalators on
the first floor of the Syrena
Tower shopping centre, the
supermarket is the go-to
shop for expats. Fivimart has
a curious mix of imported
and local wine, household
goods, fresh and packaged
food and groceries. It's likely
to be of interest to tourists for
the Western brands that can
be bought here, particularly
children's snacks, nappies,
sunscreen and toothbrushes.
You can also buy everyday
Vietnamese items to take
back home as souvenirs,
including cookware, such as
the vegetable slicers essential
for making Vietnamese
salads, and if you have room
in your luggage, the iconic
green kitchen scales that you
see at all markets (they are
accurate and fairly sturdy).
The refrigerated section gives
you a peek into the lives of
what middle-class Vietnamese
eat for dinner. You can also buy
wines from Dalat here.

POCKET TIP

Also in Syrena Tower, Annam Gourmet is a place to get good cafe and deli items.

7 EMPORIUM

172 Xuan Dieu
0936 419 346
www.emporiumhanoi.com
Open Mon–Sun 9am–8pm
[MAP p. 185 B2]

Proudly managed and run by an all-female team, Emporium has made a name for itself as a one-stop shop for fashion, homewares, souvenirs, gifts and all things south-east Asian. It's towards the To Ngoc Van end of Xuan Dieu; look for the black-and-white elephant sign and inside you'll find this bohemian treasure trove filled with jewellery, clothing, soft furnishings, trinkets, tea and coffee. The ethnic-minority textiles, such as those used in local label Future Traditions (see p. 123), are really beautiful, as are the Hmong ethnic minority cushions and bedding. Emporium promotes emerging local and expat designers and a range of handicrafts not only from Vietnam but also Myanmar, Cambodia and Laos. If you need to buy gifts to take home, Emporium has a great range at affordable prices. If you've forgotten to bring swimwear, it also stocks Western-size swimwear.

8 FUTURE TRADITIONS

17, 11/18 To Ngoc Van (call for an appointment and directions)
0904 96 2602
www.futuretraditions.asia
[MAP p. 185 A2]

Long-time expat designer Cynthia Mann has developed a real passion for fabrics produced by ethnic minority groups in Vietnam, and has forged a close working relationship with the various ethnic communities whose fabrics and workmanship she uses. Her goal is to give these crafts new life and provide sustainable income streams for the makers and their families. This relationship is apparent in the stylish clothes she respectfully produces from their fabrics. The signature jacket is her bestseller, a piece perfect for travel, and her linen pinafore dresses with ethnic-minority detailing are wonderfully comfortable in the summer heat, or with a long-sleeve top underneath for cooler weather. Future Traditions clothes are available in other stores in Hanoi, however it's worth a visit to the showroom not only to get Cynthia's expert styling advice for outfits, but also to get a glimpse of a grand villa in this luxury neighbourhood.

POCKET TIP
Contact info@futuretraditions. asia or call to visit the studio-showroom.

123

9 JOMA CAFÉ

43 To Ngọc Van
3718 6071
www.joma.biz/hanoi-vietnam
Open Mon–Sun 7am–9pm
[MAP p. 185 A1]

This American-style cafe, part of a chain found in Vietnam, Laos and Cambodia, has all the home comforts that any homesick Westerner needs. Its best-known dish, the bagel egger (it's exactly what is sounds like, a fried egg in a bagel), has soaked up many a bia hoi (street beer) hangover and its shakes, waffles and cakes are familiar for kids. Joma also has healthier dishes such as salads (the taco salad is excellent), soups and sandwiches, and hot foods such as lasagne. The fruit shakes are delicious and on a hot day the mint lemon freeze is wonderfully refreshing. On the top floor is a small, safe playground for toddlers, a godsend in a city with so few playgrounds, where parents can sit uninterrupted while using good wi-fi, in air-conditioning. There's another branch at 22 Ly Quoc Su.

10 GELATO ITALIA

31 To Ngoc Van
043 718 0014
www.gelato-italia.com
Open Mon–Sun 10am–10pm
[MAP p. 185 A1]

Hanoians love kem (ice cream), and you'll see signs advertising kem, people queuing to buy kem and kem on menus everywhere you go. Gelato Italia is equally serious about its gelati. It says it's the first authentic Italian gelati place in Hanoi, training staff with a master gelato maker. Unsurprisingly, it has been very popular, due to its creamy cones (ice cream can be icy in Hanoi) and all-natural flavours – no added preservatives, colours or flavours. This means prices are a little high by Hanoi standards (80,000VND for two scoops), but the delicious result means it's really worth it. The range of flavours is huge and changes all the time, usually including some interesting Vietnamese flavours such as young green rice, avocado and hibiscus, as well as the more traditional ones such as vanilla and chocolate. Sit outside in the lovely courtyard or upstairs and relax away from busy To Ngoc Van while you enjoy either a cone or cup, or one of the banana splits or crepes.

11 ZENITH YOGA STUDIO AND CAFE

247B Au Co
3266 8125
www.zenithyogavietnam.com
Open Mon–Fri 8am–8pm,
Sat–Sun 9am–5pm
[MAP p. 185 A1]

If the mayhem of Hanoi is all too much, Zenith Yoga Studio and Cafe may be your saviour. Both a yoga school and health-food cafe, it's a great place to come, wind down and enjoy a bit of Zen peace and gentle exercise in an air-conditioned, tranquil environment. Zenith is Hanoi's oldest yoga and pilates studio and prides itself on its international standard of instruction. The teachers all speak very good English and many are expats. They offer many different styles of yoga as well as pilates, and teacher training courses. The cafe on the ground floor has many vegan options and a good-value set menu at 150,000VND. After a class, try one of the popular chia-seed cookies, and a refreshing ginger tea, or if you're really hungry, the black bean burger and hummus.

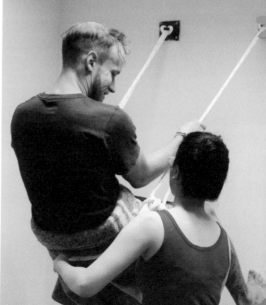

12 BIA HOI NHA HANG 68

92, 94 Quang An
Open Mon–Sun 5pm–late
[MAP p. 184 A2]

'Bia hoi' is the term used for open-air venues that serve freshly made beer from kegs, or draft beer and usually some specialty, often fried, beer snacks. This bia hoi is really a 'bia hang', an undercover restaurant that serves beer but also has an extensive menu. Enjoy the view of Ho Tay Lake (*see* p. 134) while you relax with a beer or two and good Vietnamese food. After walking past the incredible-smelling barbecue at the entrance it's hard not to order the grilled chicken, eaten dipped in the traditional sauce of lime, chilli and salt, or the roast pork. You can also enjoy other bia hoi standards such as the banana-flower salad or beef and vegetables fried with noodles. If you're feeling brave order the bun dau mam tom, fried tofu with stinky shrimp paste, it's an acquired taste but it's punchy and gives normally bland tofu a great flavour injection. Food hygiene here is important – bowls come wrapped in plastic – though the bathrooms may not reflect this.

13 FURBREW

8B/52 To Ngoc Van
0912 666736
www.furbrew.vn
Open Sun–Thurs 4–11pm,
Fri–Sat 4pm–12am
[MAP p. 185 A1]

Not surprising in the land of the bia hoi (street beer), Hanoi has gone craft beer mad. One of the most well-known brewers is Furbrew, a microbrewery that supplies high-end bars and restaurants around Hanoi. For the full Furbrew experience you can come to this Hanoi bar, which has 20-plus craft beers on tap and also in bottles. The knowledgeable young staff will help guide you through the chalkboard menu of the day's offerings or you can order flights of beer and sample a few, including locally influenced flavours such as lime leaf wheat and Bia Pho. Beer snacks can be ordered in or pop to the minimart across the road for some potato chips. If you prefer an al fresco experience, Furbrew has another location called The 100 Beer Garden. It's located across the dyke road near the flower market, set in a beer garden with bia hoi food – a little hard to find but the staff at Furbrew can order you transport to get there.

14 DON'S BISTRO

16 Quang An
3719 2828
www.dons-bistro.com
Open Mon–Sun 10am–10pm
[MAP p. 185 B3]

The huge neon lobster covering the front of this multi-level restaurant and bar gives you a good idea of the kind of establishment this is – unashamedly luxurious and a little bit old-fashioned. It's one of Hanoi's oldest high-end cocktail bars, and is run by longtime Canadian expat chef Don Berger. Don has become a bit of a local celebrity who visitors can often see smoking a cigar at the rooftop bar, enjoying a bit of live music or entertaining Vietnamese clients. Feel free to say hello! The building features a cigar room, a truffle menu and lobsters and crayfish flown in from Canada. The real attractions here are the rooftop bar with a great view of Ho Tay Lake, well-priced cocktails, good bar snacks and regular live music. The staff are friendly, speak very good English and will even help you down the many flights of stairs if you've had one too many whiskey sours.

15 HANOI ROCK CITY

27/52 To Ngọc Van
Open 24 hours
[MAP p. 185 A1]

In a city where music venues open and close with seeming regularity, Hanoi Rock City is one of the most resilient. Situated just after the minimart on To Ngoc Van, a white brick wall with the Hanoi Rock City logo masks one of the most remarkable creative spaces in Hanoi. From the entrance, look down the precarious stairs (no banister – be careful on your way out if you've had a drink or two) and you'll see a huge beer garden with a bar and some very impressive stencil art adorning the walls. HRC is many things – it has a great bandroom (it gets some impressive guests from overseas) and also has creative spaces for artists to work and display their artwork. It's also a creative hub, promoting cultural and artistic exchange. Aside from music, HRC hosts exhibitions, community activities, weekend flea markets, food festivals and many other events. Check out the Facebook page (hanoirockcity.welive) for upcoming gigs and events.

POCKET TIP
For more information on where to see live rock music around Hanoi, check out the @camaatk Facebook page

TAY HO – NGHI TAM

Located on the eastern side of Ho Tay Lake, the biggest of the many lakes in Hanoi, the Xuan Dieu and Nghi Tam areas of the Tay Ho neighbourhood contain many of the businesses where expats and wealthy Vietnamese like to eat, drink and shop.

Nghi Tam road, the very busy dyke road that stops the Red River from flooding the city (and changes its name to Au Co where it intersects Xuan Dieu street) is filled with karaoke joints, restaurants and bars. Near this junction you will find the charming 'village' of Nghi Tam, once one of most famous flower villages of Hanoi; every year many still come here to buy flowers to decorate their homes during the Tet (Lunar New Year) holiday. These days this peninsula that juts out into the lake is home to the Sheraton and Intercontinental hotels, and tiny mysterious alleys lined with huge villas and luxury apartments. Visit the beautiful Kim Lien Pagoda or take a 6am walk around Tu Hoa, the lakeside road that rings Nghi Tam village; it's a good way to get among the locals and enjoy Nghi Tam at its most peaceful. The main street, Xuan Dieu, is chaotically busy, but is full of good restaurants, cafes and bars to duck into for a break. Try to find one with a view of the lake, and enjoy relaxing out of the mayhem with a cool drink.

→ *Run by a local audiophile, this simple cafe sits next to one of the many small lakes found to the east of Ho Tay Lake*

SIGHTS & ACTIVITIES
1. Ho Tay Lake
2. Hanoi Club

SHOPPING
3. Maison de Tet Decor
4. Better World

EATING & DRINKING
5. Quan Kien
6. Oriberry
7. St Honore
8. Duy Tri
9. Red River Tea Room
10. Sunset Bar

1 HO TAY LAKE

[MAP p. 182 B2]

Formed when the Red River changed its course, Ho Tay, or West Lake, is the biggest lake in central Hanoi. Ho Tay has featured in several legends; one suggests the lake was shaped after the battle between Hung king Lac Long Quan and a nine-tailed fox spirit; another claims the original name of the lake was Golden Buffalo Lake because it was formed from the struggle of a buffalo after the disappearance of her calf. In the 11th century, it was named Foggy Lake due to its misty condition. Ultimately its name was changed to West Lake in 1573. Tay Ho is the name of a suburb that lies on its eastern banks, home to grand villas of expats and rich Hanoians, following a longtime tradition of kings of old who had their villas here. At the northern end of the lake is an old amusement park and the slightly surreal gated community of Ciputra. On a Sunday you can join Hanoi's elite, weekend road warriors in Lycra riding their super lightweight bikes.

Further around the lake, near Thuy Khue, sit rusting hulks of pleasure boats, where Hanoians once used to party. There are many beautiful temples to see around the lake including Tran Quoc Pagoda (*see* p. 96) and Phu Tay Ho (*see* p. 114). The lake is too polluted to swim in, though you'll see a few brave souls wading around on hot days. Gazing out at the lake from a cafe or restaurant or from the back of a stationary moped is a favourite Hanoian pastime. A wonderful way to explore the lake is to rent a bicycle from the **Hanoi Bicycle Collective** at 29 Nhat Chieu.

2 HANOI CLUB

76 Yen Phu
3823 8115
www.thehanoiclub.com
[MAP p. 183 D2]

In an out-of-the-way spot on the shore of Ho Tay Lake (*see* p. 134), the Hanoi Club is like a cross between a country club and a luxury hotel. Its excellent members-only facilities are available through day passes for 330,000VND on weekdays and 550,000VND on weekends. Walk into the air-conditioned lobby and buy a pass from reception, which entitles you to use the swimming pool, gym, and kids playroom. The views of Ho Tay Lake are stunning; it's pretty amazing to look out at the beautiful pagoda across the lake while you work out. There's also a small playground for toddler-aged children, a rarity in Hanoi. For an extra cost you can hit golf balls that float into the lake; just try to avoid the man in the boat who scoops them up with a net! There's also an in-house spa and for refreshments there's a restaurant and bar. The menu is extensive, with a good range of Western and Asian food. Lying next to the pool on Ho Tay with a gin and tonic and bowl of pho is a relaxing way to spend an afternoon.

3 MAISON DE TET DECOR

Villa 36 Tu Hoa, Nghi
Tam Village
www.tet-lifestyle-collection.
com/maison-de-tet-decor
Open Mon–Sun 7am–10pm
[MAP p. 185 B3]

Maison de Tet Decor is a
super stylish, comfortable
cafe housed in a huge golden
villa on the shore of Ho Tay
(see p. 134). Walk through the
relaxing courtyard; inside,
everywhere you look are
gorgeous textiles, ceramics,
sculptures and furniture,
all beautifully styled and
handcrafted with passion. This
is one of the most photogenic,
Instagrammable cafes in Hanoi
and happily the food is also
great (not surprising as it's run
by a chef and an artist). It has
healthy Western comfort food
(mostly organic), with options
including smashed avocado
and breakfast bowls (they
have gluten-free options), as
well as seasonal juices and
smoothies. They have their
own roastery where they
roast and brew international
and Vietnamese single-origin
coffees. To find it, walk up
the lake road from Xuan Dieu
past a couple of swanky
home-furnishing shops.

4 BETTER WORLD

8 Xuan Dieu
0168 639452
Open Tues–Sun 10am–7pm
[MAP p. 185 C3]

Better World is a treasure trove of products found in Vietnam and the Asian region by expat Roger Burrows – felt slippers and cashmere scarves from Mongolia, jewellery from Cambodia – the kind of items you are unlikely to see anywhere else in Hanoi. Burrows has an interesting selection of Vietnamese items too, such as fairtrade chocolate, coffee and honey, natural soaps and insect repellents, vintage art notebooks and games. The most popular items are the French-style syrups to flavour champagne, and beer from Dalat in Vietnam. The shop has a heart too – as well as ensuring the products are ethically sourced, it sells crafts made by children affected by Agent Orange, and gives 5% of profits to landmine removal in Vietnam. You'll find Better World (betterworldhanoi on Facebook) hidden up some stairs above a little dry cleaner at the southern end of Xuan Dieu.

5 QUAN KIEN

143 Nghi Tam
0978 399 983
Open Mon–Sun 9am–10.30pm
[MAP p. 183 D1]

Quan Kien seems to be either completely empty or full of rowdy, very happy Hanoians drinking their way through Quan Kien's famous rice wines and trying various exotic ethnic-minority dishes such as ants, crickets and silkworms. Have a try – deep-frying does seem to make anything taste good – but if insects don't appeal they do have more traditional dishes. In an area filled with steakhouses and karaoke joints, the glass-fronted multi-storey restaurant is on the service road a couple of metres below the dyke road of Nghi Tam, so the crowd eating on the first floor can be seen by passing traffic, adding to the celebratory atmosphere. Seating is on the floor on cushions and the tables are quite low. Staff don't speak much English but the English menu is comprehensive and has photos. The really special feature of many of these dishes is the dipping sauces that come with them, and an ideal accompaniment to any dish is the sticky rice fried in chicken fat. The famed rice wines are recommended – safe to drink, with a good range of flavours.

6 ORIBERRY

25 Xuan Dieu
6275 8669
www.oriberry.com
Open Mon–Sun 7am–11pm
[MAP p. 185 C3]

There are three great reasons to go to Oriberry – the best Western-style coffee in Hanoi, a relaxing view of Ho Tay (*see* p. 134) and an opportunity to support a successful social enterprise. The coffee is not only excellent Arabica coffee, it's fairtrade, with the beans sourced from some of Vietnam's poorest Indigenous farmers.

As well as having a cup of their coffee here, you can buy the beans to take home, along with a wide selection of beautiful ceramic cups to drink from. Oriberry is a comfortable place to just chill out and enjoy air-conditioning and wi-fi in clean, modern surrounds, or hang out on the rooftop and enjoy the view of the lake. Try the fruit salad with yoghurt and young sticky rice or the cucumber and mint juice. Like almost everywhere else in Hanoi now, they have craft beer available, along with other local beers.

7 ST HONORE

5 Xuan Dieu
3933 2355
www.sainthonore.com.vn
Open Mon–Sun 6.30am–10pm
[MAP p. 185 C3]

The French influence is most
obvious in Hanoi through
architecture and food, and
St Honore – a French bakery
in a cute little French-style
villa – has both. The huge
display of pastries and bread
that greet you upon arrival
is really the drawcard; the
wonderfully buttery, light
croissants and pain au chocolat
are outstanding, and the
breads are also very good.
Towards the back is a deli
section and a patisserie – if you
need a birthday cake while in
Hanoi, order one here and they
will deliver it to you. There
is a daily fixed-price menu,
which is usually good value,
mostly featuring traditional
French bistro food. Upstairs
the light-filled front room looks
out onto a balcony filled with
greenery with a view of Xuan
Dieu. For a secret rendezvous,
disappear into the darkened
depths of the Vietnamese-style
back room.

141

8 DUY TRI

43A Yen Phu
3829 1386
Open Mon–Sun 7am–10pm
[MAP p. 183 D2]

Chances are any Hanoi
street-food tour will include
this cafe so you can try the
famed Hanoi yoghurt coffee,
and, upstairs, the charms
of squatting on tiny chairs
in small dark spaces. To the
Vietnamese, this is exactly how
a cafe should be. Owned since
1936 by Phan Duy Sen, the
business is now run by his son
Duy Tri and his wife – have a
look at the photos of the family
dating back to the 1940s lining
the walls of the ground floor. At
the back, a tiny staircase takes
you upstairs to long thin rooms
with decorative tiled floors and
filled with an eclectic mix of
decor – a fish tank, sporting
memorabilia and fairy lights.
If it's all a bit claustrophobic,
head out to the best seat in the
house on the tiny balcony and
watch the street action. The
yoghurt coffee is a must-try
and pretty addictive, or if you'd
like something quite different,
try the fermented black sticky
rice and semi-frozen yoghurt.

9 RED RIVER TEA ROOM

Ngo So 1 Au Co, No 19 Xom
Chua, Kim Lien
Open Tues–Sun 11am–11pm,
Mon 2–11pm
[MAP p. 185 C4]

Regulars look out for local
celebrity Frank the dog at
the entrance to Tay Ho's
self-proclaimed 'mellow bar'.
After patting a very chilled-out
Frank, grab a board game
and head out past the bar to
the waterside terrace. Order
one of the local or craft beers,
such as the passionfruit beer,
served in an ice-cold beer
mug, or go local with Hanoi
beer. In the colder months find
a nook inside and sample a
dram from the huge selection
of whiskeys. The bar also
hosts Juni's Kitchen, which
serves mouth-watering
Indonesian food. The quiz
nights are full of young English
teachers and friends; check
Facebook (winepub) for
details of their events. The
bar is situated down a side
road near the entrance to the
Intercontinental Hotel – walk
past the local temple and down
a small laneway.

10 SUNSET BAR

5 Tu Hoa Cong Chua
6270 8888
www.hanoi.intercontinental.
com/sunset-bar
Open Mon–Sun 4pm–12am
[MAP p. 185 C4]

The noise and chaos of Hanoi can be hard work, so it's nice to know that at the end of a day exploring, you can retreat to this relaxing haven, set on a peaceful little archipelago on the shores of Ho Tay (*see* p. 134). The Sunset Bar at the Intercontinental features the indoor/outdoor style of lounging so popular in Bali – little cabanas that seat two, deep-set lounges and giant pouffes to put your feet on or just flop across. Dress code for guests is relaxed-casual, while elegantly attired staff glide around discreetly taking drink orders. It's a little on the pricey side, but one of their gorgeous cocktails will last through a whole Tay Ho sunset, leaving you refreshed and ready to face the mayhem of the Hanoi streets again. Signature cocktails (185,000VND) include the refreshing pomelo fizz, and the Hito, made with local rice liquor. If you feel like really treating yourself, stay for a meal or some street food–inspired bar snacks, or venture into one of the Intercontinental's restaurants for dinner.

VIETNAM MUSEUM OF ETHNOLOGY

Hanoi's best museum, the Vietnam Museum of Ethnology, is about 45 minutes in a taxi from Hoan Kiem Lake, in an area called Cau Giay. It's possible to take the 14 bus from Dinh Tien Hoang near Hoan Kiem Lake, but it's a short walk from the bus stop to the museum and very little English is spoken in this area, so only attempt this if you have a good map or mapping service on your phone.

There's not much else of interest for tourists in Cau Giay so it's testament to the reputation of the museum that so many tourists are willing to make the trek from the Old Quarter. If you have the time, it's really worth spending half a day here, especially if you have children – in a city with few playgrounds many locals and expats treat the garden area as a kids' adventure park, especially on weekends. There's a lot here; the complex consists of two museum buildings, a shop, a cafe and a huge garden filled with full-size houses taken from ethnic minority villages. The complex also houses Vietnam's main research centre that documents and preserves information on the country's 54 ethnic groups. On weekends the museum has great water puppet shows.

VIETNAM MUSEUM OF ETHNOLOGY

Nguyen Van Huyen, Cau Giay
3836 0352
Open Tues–Sun
8.30am–5.30pm

The Vietnamese Museum of Ethnology is the nearest thing Hanoi has to a theme park – think of it as an upscale, educational theme park, but without the cheesy bits. The museum is contained within a huge walled complex – there are two museum buildings, a shop, a cafe and a leafy park filled with full-size houses taken from ethnic minority villages. Buy a ticket at the front gate as you arrive and you will see the main building in front of you. This is the museum's original exhibition space and most of it highlights the country's 54 ethnic minorities. Over two floors there are exhibitions of traditional dress, handicrafts, jewellery and cooking implements. On the second floor there's also a room where kids can do art and craft activities (check the times on this so you don't miss out).

To the right of this main building is the modern Southeast Asian Culture Museum that houses exhibitions from neighbouring Asian countries, such as ethnic minority textiles and Indonesian glass painting.

The scale and presentation of the outdoor park area, full of wooden and bamboo ethnic minority houses, most of which you can enter and explore, is awe-inspiring. The houses, some up on stilts, are architecturally fascinating and many of them contain artefacts from daily life, such as sleeping mats in bedrooms, and kitchen implements. If you're here in summer come early and see this area first so you have time to see it all before the midday heat kicks in, and be sure to take mosquito repellent.

On the weekends there's a little pond where several times a day you'll see a traditional puppet show featuring puppets being manipulated with steel rods over water – check times and get tickets at the front gate.

The Craftlink shop near the entrance (*see* p. 90) is worth visiting for good-quality gifts from ethnic minority areas, soft home furnishings and trinkets.

The cafe on site serves basic food like French fries and is a good place to sit and cool down with a cold drink. If you are looking for a proper meal nearby, walk around the bottom of the lake opposite to Hem Quan restaurant (3793 9329) at 96 Chua Ha Street for some great Vietnamese food.

HALONG BAY

If there's one place in Vietnam to kick back, spend up and hang out for a couple of days, it's Halong Bay. Your first sighting of the bay's more than 1500 limestone islands rising from the endless emerald waters is one of those great moments in life when nature stuns you into stupefied, speechless submission. And this experience is followed up with countless unforgettable moments – locals selling snacks and cigarettes from fishing nets in row boats, kayaking to secluded beaches for a swim under a dramatic cliff face, touring floating fishing villages and oyster pearl farms in bamboo boats. Then, at the end of each day, you can take in the sunset from the deck of a luxury cruise boat, cocktail in hand, one of Vietnam's most memorable experiences (not to mention the cruise boats' spa treatments, seafood barbecues, and morning tai chi classes.)

I'd recommend that to ensure comfort (and safety), when booking for Halong Bay, go as high end as you can afford, and stay a night or two so that a day of bad weather doesn't ruin your visit.

A good Halong Bay cruise boat will have a knowledgable, friendly English-speaking tour guide who will inform and entertain you with the history of the bay and the lyrical myths and legends about its formation. The guides will also make sure you visit the bay's most impressive attractions (which many smaller boats skip) and will avoid some of the more polluted and crowded areas of the bay.

Must see stops include Sung Sot Cave (also known as Surprising Cave), which, despite the steep ascent, is worth visiting for its vast stage-lit interior hung with huge stalactites; Luon Cave for kayaking and meeting the monkeys that live around the cave; Ti Top beach for a swim and beautiful views of the bay; and the floating villages where you can buy seafood from the fishermen, and have it cooked onboard for your dinner that night. Cat Ba Island, with its extensive national park, is only really worth exploring if you're a keen hiker and wildlife enthusiast.

The Halong Bay area is a UNESCO World Heritage Site and once you get there and see its incredible topography you'll understand why.

The limestone islands, or 'karsts', many featuring huge caves, natural arches and small lakes, are remarkable not just for having been formed by

nature, but also for how little they have been affected by humans. The many tourists and the families who live in floating villages on the bay are all restricted by government laws designed to protect the site.

A trip to Halong Bay from Hanoi takes four hours each way by car or bus, another reason to stay overnight. Avoid staying in the town of Halong, which offers little in the way of either beauty or entertainment. The most spectacular (and expensive) way to travel to Halong is by seaplane, which takes 30 minutes. It's easy to book cruises and transfers in one of the travel agencies around Hang Be in Hanoi, or online. Try Handspan (handspan.com) which emphasizes responsible tourism; Bhaya cruises (bhayacruises.com), which seems to have the biggest fleet of reliable cruise boats on the bay and a good range of prices to choose from; or Buffalo Tours (buffalotours.com), an established, well-liked tour company with staff who know the area well.

When packing for Halong, make sure you take mosquito repellent, bottled water, a hat, swimwear and comfortable shoes – the best views and some of the caves do require some hiking, often in steep terrain.

BAT TRANG

The trick with a trip to Bat Trang village, the pottery village on the banks of the Red River, is to know when to leave – sure, shop around a bit before buying, but try to make a few purchases before it becomes all too much and you have to go. Walking around, often in the stifling heat, looking at pottery shop after pottery shop can become overwhelming and claustrophobic, but it is worth the trip, not just to buy pottery but to see how a village where 90 per cent of the village's inhabitants are involved in some way with pottery making, selling or distribution.

The trip out here is not just about shopping; it's also fascinating to see the workshops where workers make the pottery, and the staff don't seem to mind you watching as long as you stay at a respectful distance. It's quite mesmerising to see the concentration as a young man delicately paints classic white glazed vases with blue dragons and other symbols from Chinese mythology, while next to him a colleague paints cherry blossoms onto a Japanese teapot.

BAT TRANG

Bat Trang consists of a main, central street that is lined with pottery shops. There is also a large pottery market off to one side. Turn left from the main street and there are pottery painting workshops for kids, or anyone really, with plain pieces of pottery ready to be painted and fired. Further up, Bat Trang Pagoda is a beautiful place to visit.

Bat Trang was established in either the 10th or 11th century, around the time Hanoi was founded, and due to its clay soil, soon became home to many potters who built kilns and sold pottery to boats passing on the Red River. Bat Trang is now the place where Hanoians get their ceramic goods, from tableware to statues of gods for their altars to garden pots, and is so full of displays of piled-high pottery, it really has to be seen to be believed. After seeing shop after shop stacked high with pottery, and a few of the factories, you become an expert in identifying different styles and materials – delicate Japanese tea sets, big chunky blue and white Chinese vases, modern functional Western-style dinner sets, terracotta tiles and more. Staff at the main shops are adept at wrapping your purchases for transport and the woven hemp bags they put each purchase in are a bonus.

To get there, hire a taxi or take bus 47 from Long Bien, then get a taxi back with your shopping. What used to be a trip out to a town in the countryside is now a 30-minute drive to suburban Hanoi, thanks to the city's rapid expansion; the village is surrounded by just enough rural land that it can still be called the countryside.

One good way to see Bat Trang is to find a combined tour to the Van Phuc silk village (either online or through one of the agents on Hang Be). You get to sit in an air-conditioned bus to both villages, have a tour guide show you around and help you barter, maybe make your own vase, and leave your purchases on the bus while your guide takes you to a local restaurant for lunch. Finding a restaurant without having a guide to order food in Bat Trang is hard, so it's worth eating before you go.

If you want to send your pottery home, postage from Hanoi is not too expensive and generally safe. Head to the international post office at 75 Dinh Tien Hoang next to Hoan Kiem Lake with your package unsealed – they will need to inspect the contents.

⌡APA

Arriving in the hillside town of Sapa after a few days in Hanoi is literally a breath of fresh air. The train from Hanoi takes eight hours, but you'll know it was worth it when you arrive to find soaring views, beautiful stepped rice-paddy fields cut into the side of the Hoang Lien Son mountains, and villagers in traditional clothes lining the streets of the town.

To get there from Hanoi take the train from Ga Hanoi to Lao Cai, then it's about a 50-minute drive on the winding roads by taxi to Sapa. Many travellers prefer to make it an overnight train journey in a sleeper cabin, so you can sleep through most of it. Or you can shorten your journey by taking a private car with a driver, or a bus with reclining seats from Hanoi, both which take about five hours. Buses travel during the day, so you will get to see more of northern Vietnam's scenery along the way.

Most visitors use Sapa as a base to explore the region. You can go climbing on Vietnam's highest mountain, Fansipan; visit nearby Thac Bac waterfall, take a motorbike tour of surrounding areas, and visit villages of the Hmong, Dao, Giay, Pho, Lu and Tay ethnic minorities. These different minorities can be identified by their dress – for example the black Hmong wear deep indigo embroidered dresses and turbans and can be visited in nearby Cat Cat Village (among others), while the red Dao wear more colourful clothing topped by a red turban decorated with coins. It's fascinating to see how they blend their traditions with modern life – seeing a woman in traditional dress pull out a mobile phone can be quite surreal.

One of the most popular activities is to trek through rice-paddy fields to a nearby ethnic minority village and stay overnight in a homestay where your host will cook you some of their special dishes, take you on a tour of the village and surrounds, and show you where to buy some ethnic minority handicrafts. People will approach you in town offering these tours. You can also do all of these activities on your own, in a day. For example, Ta Phin village is a four- to five-hour trek away; when you get there you can soothe your tired body at the **Red Dao Spa** – just make sure

you have the name written down and a villager will point out how to get there. You can also get a taxi there from Sapa, a 40-minute drive with great views.

If you're not a climber (climbers are advised to find a good tour guide and porters in town) and want to visit the summit of Fansipan, you can take the new cable car, which takes 20 minutes and costs around 700,000VND for the cable car and funicular railway.

In the evenings in Sapa, check out Quang Trong Square and see locals doing exercises, hoverboarding and catching up. On Saturday nights the 'love market' sees youths come in from surrounding areas to flirt, dance, sing and play flutes. On a really foggy day, when it's not worth leaving the town, there are still plenty of things to do – sign up for a cooking class at **The Hill Station** (37 Fansipan), walk down to **Hieu Stone** in Cat Cat village for a stone carving workshop or treat yourself to an upmarket massage at the **Victoria Resort & Spa** (Xuan Vien Street) in the centre of town.

EAT & STAY

Have a drink at **The H'mong Sisters** (31 Muong Hoa), or try **Maison de Sapa** (18 Thac Bac) which has home-cooked Vietnamese food and great views of Fansipan mountain. Try the barbecue skewers at **Co Lich** (1 Pansipan), or visit The Hill Station hotel's **Signature Restaurant** (37 Fansipan) for its great fusion food. At Victoria Resort & Spa's **Ta Van Restaurant** (Xuan Vien Street), although the hotel itself appears like a gorgeous Swiss chalet, the restaurant offers a range of Vietnamese and western dishes at the higher end of the price scale.

For a laidback joint that has shisha, cheap cocktails and even their own specialty drink (banana wine) try **Color Bar** (56 Fansipan), a timber shack with a cobblestone terrace. After a trek, warm up in the **Mountain Bar and Pub** (4 Muong Hoa) to sit in front of the fire with some warm apple wine or an egg coffee.

If you're looking to completely get away from any remnants of urban life, social enterprise **Sapa O'Chau** (8 Thac Bac) is Vietnam's first ethnic minority owned and operated tour company, offering both guided treks and homestays in villages in the area. There are a number of other great homestay options in the surrounding region.

At the pricier end of the scale, **Topas Ecolodge** (Than Kim), located 18km (11mi) outside of Sapa, aims to have a minimal impact on the environment. Although the stone huts where guests stay are free from TVs or wifi, they do offer air conditioning, a rain shower or huge stone bathtub.

∫HOPPING

Shopping in Sapa is all about ethnic minority handicrafts, textiles and silver trinkets. Everywhere you go in this region you will be approached by street vendors selling ethnic minority merchandise, which are generally good quality and not too expensive. If you're looking to shop in a more controlled environment, the tourist shops in the centre of Sapa have a good selection of things to buy, but are a bit more expensive. For ethnic minority textiles and handicrafts try **Indigo Cat** (46 Fansipan), **Wild Orchid** (29 Cau May) or **Sapa O'Chau** (8 Thac Bac) that specialises in Hmong handicrafts; for jewellery try **Sapa Silver** (19 Muong Hoa).

You can also go to markets in nearby towns. **Can Cau Market** on a Saturday is the best of these; it's a three-hour drive from Sapa to not only buy but see locals in amazing clothes who've travelled in to Can Cau to buy their food and clothing.

163

LOCALS AND EXPERTS

NGA HOANG AND LIEM TRAN

Journalist Nga and travel photographer Liem own Collective Memory – the House of Curios (*see* p. 56)

What is your favourite season?

While summer in Hanoi is very sticky and winter is very biting, autumn is obviously my favourite season. We enjoy walking around the lakes and cooking with what the season has to offer. The cha com (green sticky rice pork roll) is to die for.

What is your favourite place to eat?

Chim Sao (*see* p. 44) is our all-time favourite and the go-to place whenever we have out-of-town guests. The setting is nostalgic and the food is homey. All the dishes are tapas-style and cooked with great care and passion.

What is your favourite drink?

Caphe trung (egg coffee) is such a wonderful invention. I think it's the Vietnamese interpretation of the Italian capuccino.

What is your favourite specialty food?

Cha ca (Hanoi-styled grilled fish), for me, sums up perfectly the Hanoian cuisine which is best known for its subtlety. It's a special treat for guests too.

What is your favourite creative space?

Hanoi Social Club (*see* p. 76) is the kind of place where you can chill out, read books and enjoy some live music. It serves wonderful vegan-friendly dishes too.

What is your favourite shop?

Module 7 (*see* p. 116) showcases the very best of upscale handcrafted products from Vietnam ranging from hand-dyed fashion pieces to bamboo wallets.

Where do you go to relax?

Hanoi is a city that is bestowed with lakes. West Lake (Ho Tay) (*see* p. 134) is one of my favourite hang-out areas. There's no better way of relaxing than strolling around the West Lake and kicking back with a coffee at a lakeside cafe and watching the sun go down.

CYNTHIA MANN

Fashion designer, owner of Future Traditions (*see* p. 123)

What is your favourite season?

I love the blue skies and sunshine of autumn. It's the best time of year to go cycling around West Lake (Ho Tay) (*see* p. 134) and out into the countryside close to Hanoi.

What is your favourite place to eat?

I think that has to be Mau Dich (State-run Food Shop no 37; *see* p. 104), the coupon restaurant, in Truc Bach. Home-style Vietnamese cooking soaking up the nostalgia of post-war 1976 – love the food and the decor.

What is your favourite speciality food?

I love banh cuon, delicious steamed rice pancakes. I've been going to a little hole-in-the-wall place since I first visited Hanoi in 2003. It's on Bao Khanh near the corner of Hang Hanh. It's still going strong and has expanded from tiny to small!

What is your favourite drink?

There is nothing more refreshing than sitting on a small stool at one of the many street vendors having a glass of mia da (icy sugarcane juice with a dash of cumquat) to quench your thirst. There's one just opposite Cho Hom (*see* p. 42), the fabric market, that is my regular.

What is your favourite creative space?

The Future Traditions studio/ showroom (*see* p. 123) off To Ngoc Van is the perfect creative working space. Part studio and part showroom, it's light and airy and I'm surrounded by the textiles that inspire my collections.

What is your favourite shop?

My obsession is ethnic minority textiles and culture so no surprises that my favourite shop is 54 Traditions (*see* p. 98). I love exploring the five floors of artefacts, textiles, carvings, tools and shamanism, and being inspired by Nhung and Mark's extraordinary knowledge about these people and their cultures.

Where do you buy your fabric?

For commercially produced fabrics Cho Hom (*see* p. 42) and Nhin Hiep, and for all the ethnic textiles I buy direct from the communities that make them. The Craftlink Bazaar held every November is a great opportunity to meet the makers and buy an amazing range of textiles.

Where do you go to relax?

Yakushi for a massage or if I'm feeling more energetic, I ask our friend Dan (Around Hanoi) to take us off the beaten track to explore the countryside on the outskirts of the Hanoi.

VAN CONG TU

Streetfood tour guide and Instagram food star (@vietnamesegod)

What is your favourite season?

Autumn, though autumn in Hanoi is much like summer everywhere else. Custard apples, pomelos and persimmons are all rolling around the streets, being sold by vendors wheeling bicycles. It's much more pleasant to dine outside in autumn, perfect for beers and snacks by one of the lakeside bia hoi (street beer) restaurants.

What is your favourite place to eat?

Because I eat out so much for work, I have to say home. Doing a morning shop at the market, putting the rice cooker on, dipping some boiled pork in fish sauce and chili, leafy greens simply stir-fried, maybe another vegetable dish, a sweet and sour fish broth, some pickled bitter cabbage on the side. A few mangosteens or freshly cut watermelon to finish. I could eat a variation on that every day.

What is your favourite specialty food?

Bun rieu cua is a fresh rice noodle dish with crab paste, sometimes tofu, perhaps a cut of pork sausage or some beef, even a couple of snails are possibilities at some vendors.

It's all served in a sour tomato broth, with tons of herbs on the side, and a big dollop of chili paste on top. Pungent fermented shrimp paste – optional.

What is your favourite drink?

Nuoc sau, which is a seasonal drink available in the summer. It's made from a hard green fruit (loosely translated as apricot, but not really) with sour properties that gets steeped in syrup. The fruit and a spoonful of syrup gets served in a tall glass, sometimes the sau is muddled, then filled to the top with iced water. Cools the body on a sweaty hot summer day.

What is the most Instagrammable dish in Hanoi?

I pretty much post a photo of everything I eat to Instagram but when I go through my feed, I see lots of images of pho, which only stands to reason. It's originally a northern dish, originating not far from Hanoi, and I eat a lot of it. Probably everyone with an Instagram account who visits Hanoi has pho in their feed.

TRAVEL TIPS

GETTING TO HANOI

Flying to Hanoi

Noi Bai Airport has both domestic
(Terminal 1) and international (Terminal 2)
terminals with shuttle buses between them.

Noi Bai Airport
Phu Minh, Soc Son
3886 5047
Code: HAN
www.hanoiairportonline.com

Getting to/from Noi Bai Airport

- Local buses are the slowest option and
  neither bus goes right into the centre
  around Hoan Kiem Lake, so only do this
  if you're really on a budget. (The cost of a
  taxi to take you the rest of the way and it
  may not be worth it.)

- Bus 7 goes to the Kim Ma area via the
  west side of Ho Tay Lake and is good if
  you're staying in west Ba Dinh or around
  the Lotte Tower.

- Bus 17 travels along the Red River to Long
  Bien bus station and from there it's a short
  taxi or bus ride to Truc Bach, Tay Ho or
  the Old Quarter and Hoan Kiem Lake.

- Jetstar and Vietnam Airlines have buses
  that drop you close to Hoan Kiem Lake for
  30,000VND.

- You can book a taxi in advance
  with Hanoi Airport Transfers (www.
  hanoitransferservice.com) or use one of
  the official airport Noi Bai taxis (3886 5615)
  that you find outside the terminal for about
  350,000-400,000VND. Do not take other
  taxis that offer you a fixed price.

Train to Hanoi

The train from Ho Chi Minh City to Hanoi,
the Reunification Express, passes through
a number of towns on the way up the
coast. Straight through from HCMC to
Hanoi takes approximately 34 hours, but
the journey can be broken with stops at the
towns along the way. There are four trains
a day on this route. If you're on one of the
early arrivals and it's too early to check
into your hotel, head up to Tong Duy Tan
(a 10-minute walk or take a taxi) where there
are two 24-hour cafes – Puku and Xofa Café
(see p. 75) – where you can happily relax
(and even sleep) for a few hours.

GETTING AROUND HANOI

Walking

Hanoi is small enough that walking is an
ideal way to get to know the city. The
biggest challenge for tourists is figuring out
how to cross the road. The trick is to walk
slowly and purposefully across the road – no
sudden moves – so that oncoming traffic can
see you early and move around you. If this
seems too hard, find a local who is about to
cross and cross with them.

Bus

Hanoi's public bus system is great, once
you get used to its idiosyncrasies (buses
sometimes don't stop so you need to leap
onto a moving vehicle) and bus etiquette is
strict – don't be noisy, do what the conductor
says and get on and off quickly.

Buy a ticket for trips around central Hanoi
for 7000VND from the roaming conductor.
Bus stops are quite far apart so be prepared
for a walk if you miss your stop. For more
information, including a bus map, go to
www.tramoc.com.vn and click on 'Tieng
Anh' for English.

Taxi

- Hanoi's taxis are relatively cheap and
  reliable, if you use the right firms.

- If any driver offers you a fixed price to a
  destination, don't get in; though if you're
  stuck and there's none of the reliable taxi
  firms around, and no guard or concierge
  to call one for you, you may have to just
  agree and take the more expensive taxi.

- Late nights are a time to be particularly wary, particularly if you are visibly intoxicated.
- Small and medium-size taxis are generally cheaper than a seven-seater.
- Reliable firms: Hanoi Taxi and Taxi CP (3853 5353), ABC Taxis (3719 1919), Mai Linh/Open (3833 3333), Thanh Nha (3821 5215)

Uber / Grab

Hanoi has both Uber and a local version called Grab. Both are reliable and work by downloading an app, then booking a trip with it. The app then gives you the license plate of your driver and a set price for the fare. In Vietnam you can pay drivers either with the app or in cash, however Grab requires a local phone number. Grab also has motorbike taxis and they supply helmets.

Xe oms, cyclos & motorbikes

- Travelling on any form of motorbike may void your travel insurance, so be sure to check this on your policy.
- Be careful of the 'Hanoi tattoo' – a burn from the exhaust pipes of motorbikes, particularly if you are in a traffic jam.
- With a xe om (motorbike taxi), fix a price to your destination before you get on.
- As a tourist, you take a risk hiring and riding a motorbike in Hanoi as the traffic and idiosyncratic road rules take quite a while to get used to. If you don't ride a motorbike in your home country it is not recommended you start riding in Vietnam.
- A cyclo (three-wheeled bicycle taxi) is a great way to see central Hanoi, especially if you want to take photos. When hiring one, be sure to fix a price before you get in.

Bicycle

Cycling is a great way to see a bit more of Hanoi. You can hire bikes at the Hanoi Bicycle Collective near the dragon sculptures on the west side of Ho Tay Lake (*see* p. 134). You can take a day trip around the lake (about 17km), though it can be a little scary during peak hour. There are bicycle tours around the rose and market gardens, and through villages and rural areas near Hanoi, mostly near the Red River, with experienced cycling tour guide Dan Tran (www.aroundhanoi.com).

MONEY

- The Vietnamese currency is the dong, or VND.
- There are many international ATMs such as ANZ, Citibank and HSBC. With the exchange rate you will be a millionaire, but some ATMs only allow you to take out 2 million at a time, which may not go that far. Many ATMs will allow you to withdraw 5 million from a foreign account, with fewer exchange-rate costs.
- If you are in town during Tet (Lunar New Year), ATMs have occasionally been known to run out of money (though this happens less and less now), so don't wait until you're down to your last dong to cash up.
- It can be useful to carry a small amount of US dollars as some places will accept this and it is easy to change at a bank or in the gold shops.

VI-FI

When you get to Vietnam you can buy a cheap local SIM card with data from Vinaphone. You may need a Vietnamese person to help you set it up. If you don't buy one, virtually every cafe and restaurant in Hanoi except bia hois (beer stalls) has good wi-fi. Look around for the password on a wall nearby or on a menu, or ask a waiter.

There aren't many internet cafes so you'll want to have a wi-fi enabled device. If you don't and you're desperate, try getting online at one of the travel agencies/cafes you see in the area west of Ly Quoc Su or on Hang Be, or the business centre at an upmarket hotel.

PUBLIC HOLIDAYS & FESTIVALS

An increasing number of locals are travelling on these short breaks, so it is worth checking dates and booking ahead to ensure your travel plans go smoothly; search for Vietnam on www.officeholidays.com.

New Year's Day January 1

Tet (Lunar New Year) End of January or early February. This is the big Vietnamese holiday each year. Once it was the quietest time of the year, but most tourist places are open these days. The week itself is still relatively quiet with many shops and most sightseeing attractions closed. Local travel (and traffic) is very busy in the run-up to Tet, so make sure you book any flights/transport/accommodation well ahead of time.

Hung King's Temple Festival Tenth day of the third lunar month (usually sometime in April)

Reunification Day April 30

Labour Day May 1

National Day September 2. This is becoming a big celebration, though it's quieter than Tet.

TEMPLES & SHRINES

It's not always apparent, but Vietnam is a fairly conservative country in terms of clothing: shoulders are usually covered and necklines are high. This is important to note when visiting temples. Shorts and skirts should be to the knees at least, and your shoulders should be covered. Some temples will have something they can lend you if you are uncovered.

If you see shoes at the entrance to a temple, remove yours and leave them there (no one will take your shoes). Talking is permitted, but do it quietly. It's generally okay to take photos, but be respectful of worshippers who are there for spiritual reasons.

Temples and pagodas are always especially busy on the first and 15th days of the lunar month.

SHOPPING

Old Quarter

The origins of the 36 streets of Hanoi's Old Quarter are as old as the 13th century, when skilled craftspeople migrated to the city and the artisan guilds they formed filled entire streets with their workshops and wares. These are slowly disappearing, but are still reflected today in the names of the streets. Some remain true to their origins, like Hang Dong (brass street) and Hang Gai (silk street), but even in the streets being taken over by new modern fashion shops and restaurants you will still find examples of these original trades in small, family-run artisan businesses. Look for Hang Bac (silver products), Hang Ma (paper products) and Hang Go (wood products), just to name a few.

Shopping tips

- Hanoi's not always a great place for bargaining, which is frustrating if you're used to it or even see it as a sport.

- The best shopping area for souvenirs and Western-sized clothing is around Nha Tho near the cathedral, with plenty of places to refresh yourself in between.

- Apart from the usual souvenirs you'll see everywhere – traditional lacquerware, silk purses and bags – there are some other interesting Hanoi purchases: Thuong Dinh badminton shoes in Western sizes, foot badminton shuttlecocks, Goretex/North Face jackets, seconds of high-end clothing labels (sometimes available at Made In Vietnam shops, *see* p. 43), locally grown Fairtrade Arabica coffee and a one-cup drip filter device, clothing made from ethnic minority fabric, modern Vietnamese art, and vintage-style maps.

Convenience stores

Mini marts, mini supermarkets that sell Western and Vietnamese goods, are slowly being replaced by more Western-style convenience stores that have a much smaller selection of food but also sell hot snacks.

LANGUAGE

- Most Vietnamese appreciate any effort made to speak their language, so knowing a few words goes a long way. It's a tonal language, with six different tones, so it can be quite hard for a Westerner to learn.

- Vietnamese is written using the Roman alphabet so you can get an approximation of the language without too much effort, but unless you learn the tones and the associated accents, it's easy to make mistakes. There are words that look the same but have very different meanings when different tones are applied: for example, bạn=friend, bàn=table, bận=busy and bán=sell.

- It's important to note that there are strong regional differences in accent and dialect, particularly between the north and south, so if you're aiming to learn some Vietnamese before you come here, make sure it's the right accent you are learning.

- You may recognize some words that come from French such as ga (train station, from *gare*), vang (wine, from *vin*) and bo (butter, from *beurre*). Some of the older generation still speak French and may enjoy doing so for nostalgic reasons.

Phrase Guide

Hello (general greeting for anytime of the day) – xin chao (sin chow)

Goodbye – tam biet (tam bee-yet)

I don't understand Vietnamese – toi khong hieu tieng Viet (toy khong hugh tyeng vee-et)

Please – xin lam on (sin larm uhrn)

Thank you – xin cam on (sin gahm ern)

Excuse me – xin loi (sin loy)

How much is this? – bao nhieu tien (bow nyow tee-en)

Cheers – Mot hai ba (mot hi ba)

Can I have the bill please? – Tin tien (ting tee-en)

Straight ahead – di thang (dee tarng)

Turn left – re trai (se chai)

Turn right – re phai (se fiy)

Stop here – dung o day (zung a day)

Wait five minutes – cho nam phut (cho nam foot)

BUSINESS CHANGES

Due to issues with building leases, shops and cafes in Hanoi can close suddenly. So if you're travelling to an area for a specific business, it's best to check if the business still exists at that address. English is not necessarily widely spoken by hospitality and retail staff, so do this via their social media pages or website. Around holiday seasons such as Tet, you might also want to ask your hotel concierge or a Vietnamese contact (even a tour guide) to call and check opening hours.

RECOMMENDED HOTELS

Hanoi Club (www.thehanoiclub.com)

Apricot Hotel (www.apricothotels.com)

Paloma Hotel (www.hanoipalomahotel.com)

La Siesta Hotel Trendy (www. hanoilasiestatrendyhotel.com; avoid rooms without exterior windows)

Cinnamon Hotel (https://cinnamonhotel.net)

ARTS SCENE

Hanoi has always had an interesting and dynamic arts scene, and this has been given an avant garde edge by young artists, musicians and writers who've travelled and studied internationally. Artist-run bars and cafes such as Manzi (*see* p. 109), Tadioto (*see* p. 37) and Hanoi Rock City (*see* p. 131) are hubs for the arts scene, as are more established venues such as the Hanoi Opera House (*see* p. 26) and L'Espace (*see* p. 25).

Check out www.hanoigrapevine.com to find out what's happening around town when you're there, as well as the social media pages for the venues listed. Friends of Vietnam Heritage (www.fvheritage.org) also list arts and cultural events such as traditional music performances, walking tours and art workshops.

TOURS

Hang Be in the Old Quarter is full of travel agents that offer reputable tours of Hanoi. If you want something a bit different (but still reputable!) here are some options:

- Sophie's Art Tours (www.sophiesarttour. com) are tours of Hanoi's galleries and museums.
- Duyen's Market Tours (www.chefduyen. com) are tours of Hanoi's markets and cooking classes with Hanoi chef Duyen.
- Hanoi Street Food Tours (www.street foodtourshanoi.blogspot.com.au) are customised street-food tours around Hanoi.
- Around Hanoi (www.aroundhanoi.com) are bicycle tours around the rural area near Hanoi, mostly down near the Red River.
- Hanoi Kids (www.hanoikids.org) are free tours with students keen to practice their English.

SPAS & MASSAGE

One of the great joys of Hanoi is access to inexpensive massages, manicures and hairdressers. The best of these is a hair wash with up to an hour of head massage for around $10.

If you're staying in a hotel with a spa it's a good idea to go there even though it's likely to be more expensive, so you can wander back up to your room afterwards and relax in post-treatment bliss – wandering out into Hanoi traffic in a daze can be quite dangerous! Some recommended places are listed below; otherwise find one at a nearby hotel or ask your hotel concierge/receptionist for a recommendation.

- Yakushi (Tay Ho; 3719 1971) has massage booths separated by curtains. Bookings essential.
- Lancy Spa (Tay Ho; 3719 9461) does haircuts with head massages, as well as body massages, pedicures, waxing and facials.
- Hanoi La Belle Spa (Hoan Kiem; 6686 9163)

ETIQUETTE

Northern Vietnamese people are said to be resilient, proud and determined – surely helpful character traits for those who have had to repel so many invaders throughout their history.

- As in many parts of South-east Asia, 'face' is important to Vietnamese people. Try to avoid doing anything that means people 'lose face', such as losing your temper or reprimanding someone publically.
- Vietnamese society is very much based around family and the Vietnamese love children, so asking about family is a good way to connect, show respect and be polite. Confucian philosophy means that elders are much more respected than in the West, so an elder will often be served first at dinner or in a shop.
- The polite way to pass money, credit cards, and food on tables is with both hands. Try to avoid: public displays of affection, touching anyone's head or shoulders, or using your finger to point (use your whole hand). Also avoid standing with your hands on your hips or crossing your arms in front of your chest.
- When eating you will normally be given chopsticks and a flat spoon. Hold the bowl close to your face and use chopsticks to place food in your mouth. If you can't use chopsticks it's okay to ask for a fork. When you're finished place the chopsticks flat on top of the bowl.

CLOTHING

Unless you are planning to take taxis everywhere you go, do not bring your best shoes to Hanoi. Due to the extremes of weather, your shoes will possibly melt (really), dissolve in tropical floodwaters or fall apart because of the harshness of footpaths. A pair of sports shoes for walking, boots in winter and high-soled slides in summer, as well as a pair of nicer shoes for when you go out to a higher-end place, should suffice.

Summer clothing should be cotton and loose for casual events, and a nice shirt is good for evening wear. Remember you can buy Western-size North Face, Gore-Tex and puffer jackets really cheaply.

HEALTH

Vaccinations are recommended against diphtheria, hepatitis A, tetanus and typhoid, and you may also consider cholera, hepatitis B, Japanese encephalitis and rabies, depending on where you are going. Some of these vaccinations need to be done weeks before you go, so good planning is necessary. Some areas of Hanoi and surrounds can have dengue fever (check with your travel doctor) so long-sleeved cotton shirts are advised to avoid mosquito bites.

As with many other major cities in Asia, air quality is an issue. Take or buy a pollution mask if you're going to be walking around a lot or riding on motorbikes or taxis. Nasal saline sprays are helpful for those with allergies and can be bought from pharmacies (nhà thuoc) relatively cheaply.

DRINKS

One of the joys of drinking in Hanoi is going to a bia hoi, an outdoor pub that serves fresh low-alcohol beer and beer snacks. Bia hoi is also the name of the fresh beer they serve and it's worth trying, as are the local beers Truc Bach Beer and Hanoi Beer. Craft beer has become huge in recent years – try Furbrew (*see* p. 129) or Pasteur Street (*see* p. 67).

Wine can be expensive but spirits, cocktails and beer are fairly cheap. There's a cocktail revolution going on and Hanoi is full of proud mixologists, whipping up classics and new creations. As in Bali and Thailand, be careful of drinking spirits in lower-end places as the alcohol might have been adulterated.

Vietnamese green tea contains a lot of caffeine (as does their coffee), so be careful how much you drink. Vietnamese rice wine should be tried but stick to higher-end establishments such as Highway 4 (*see* p. 19) restaurants (which sell the Son Tinh brand).

FOOD

For many visitors Hanoi street food is a highlight of their trip; some come just for that reason. The most famous dish is pho, the fragrant rice noodle soup flavoured with spices (Pho Huyen, *see* p. 105). Hanoi pho is very different to the southern version – Hanoi's version has the aroma of star anise and the subtle flavours of a clean broth.

Bun cha is another favourite – marinated and grilled pork patties and pork belly, served with noodles, fresh herbs and a dipping sauce (Bun Cha Hang Than, *see* p. 106). You'll know a bun cha restaurant by the incredible smells floating in a cloud of smoke towards you around lunchtime.

Other great dishes to try include pho cuon, steamed rolled rice noodles stuffed with pork or mushrooms (Pho Cuon Hung Ben, *see* p. 108), and xoi, sticky rice served with a variety of toppings (Xoi Yen, *see* p. 13). Com binh danh is a kind of Vietnamese buffet where a variety of dishes are kept in bain maries and you can choose a few dishes to have with rice.

There are few street-food establishments listed in this book as places open and close frequently and one location may serve one dish in the morning, a different one at lunch and a different one again on the weekends.

Many middle-class Hanoians favour restaurants over street food due to perceived hygiene concerns – two restaurants that have fairly comprehensive menus of Hanoi street food (as well as regional food) in a restaurant environment are Quan An Ngon (*see* p. 32) and Nha Hang Ngon (*see* p. 31). New Day (*see* p. 14) is a restaurant that serves com bin danh.

If you're concerned about hygiene, do remember that a dirty floor is not a sign of an unhygienic establishment. At a street food stall, bia hoi (street beer stall) or even a restaurant it is customary to throw used napkins, paper and peanut shells on the floor for staff to clean up later.

It's always best to choose a place that's busy with locals, and if in doubt it's good to ask your hotel or guide for recommendations on where to eat. Try to eat as close to lunchtime as possible (between 11.30am and midday) so you can get fresh food.

I

B

C

CHULA
⊕

HANOI
BICYCLE
COLLECTIVE

TÂY HỒ

*Hồ Tây
(West Lake)*

184——

TỪ LIÊM

2

VIETNAM
MUSEUM OF
ETHNOLOGY
⊕ (BẢO TÀNG DÂN
TỘC HỌC VIỆT NAM)

BA ĐÌNI

3

**CẦU
GIẤY**

LOTTE
OBSERVATION
DECK
⊕

CAFÉ
CCCP
O

HÀ NỘI

4

A

B

C

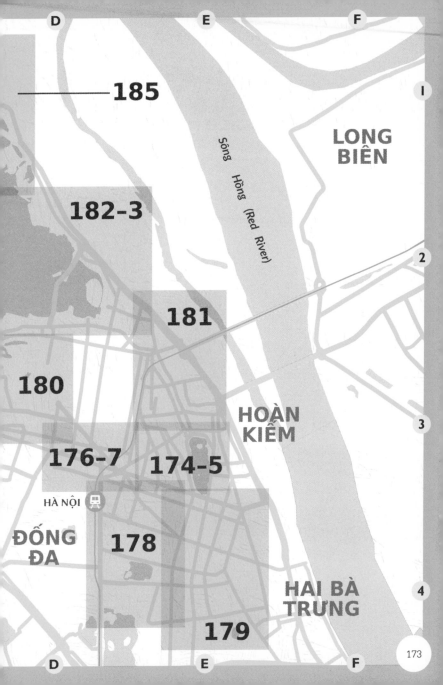

A

TRANQUIL BOOKS AND COFFEE

PHUNG HUNG

CỬA ĐÔNG

NGUYỄN VĂN TỐ

TRÂM

NGÕ

Rising Dragon Estate Hotel

Golden Cyclo Hotel

HÀ TRUNG

BỒNG

HÀNG DA

HÀNG

HANOI SOCIAL CLUB

HỘI VŨ

QUÁN SỨ

HÀNG BÔNG

TRÀNG

THI

QUÁN SỨ

B

HÀNG

NÓN

HÀNG GAI

Hanoi Trendy Hotel & Spa

Hanoi Charming Hotel

Thu Giang Guesthouse

Nhà Hát Tuồng Việt Nam (Vietnam Tuong Theatre)

Tung Trang Hotel

HÀNG MÀNH

HÀNG BÔNG

LOADING T

MADAME HIEN

CHÂN CẨM

DƯỜNG THÀNH

PHÙ DOÃN

JOMA CAFÉ

PIZZA 4P'S

HUYỆN

MAD BOTANIST– THE GIN SPECIALIST

NGÕ

BANH CUON BA HANH

CINNAMON HOTEL

ST JOSEPH'S CATHEDRAL (Nhà Thờ Lớn)

PASTEUR STREET BREWING

PORTE D'ANNAM

PHÙ DOÃN

HANOI SMILE

Vườn Hoa Hàng Trống

N

0   100 m

TRẦN HƯNG ĐẠO

TRÀNG

THI

C

HÀNG QUAT

Golden Sun Suites Hotel

TAN MY DESIGN

PHỐ HÀNG GAI

GINKG

Golden Silk Boutique Hotel

TSNO BOUTIQU

TIRED CITY

The Palm Hotel Sp

HÀNG

LÝ QUỐC SỬ

LE PETIT BRUXELLES

NAGU

TRÔNG

CAFÉ RUNAM

MA

PHỐ

CHULA

VAN YEN ART CAFE

1

2

3

4

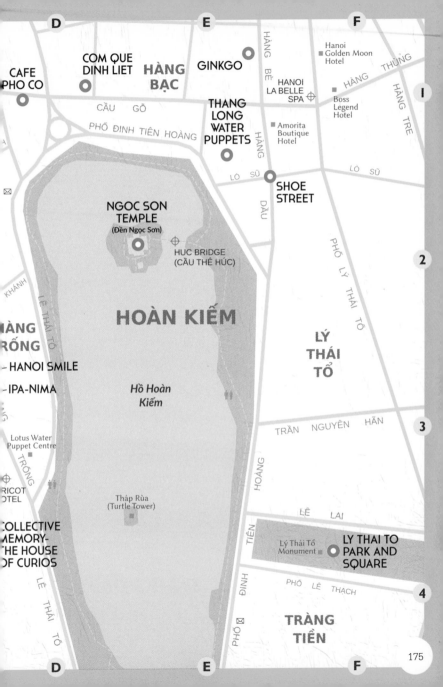

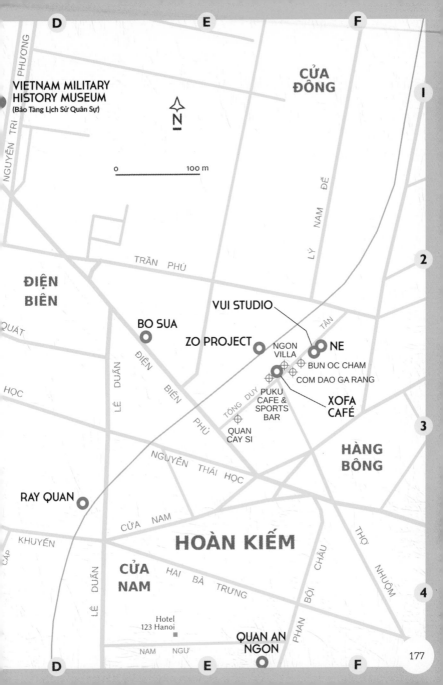

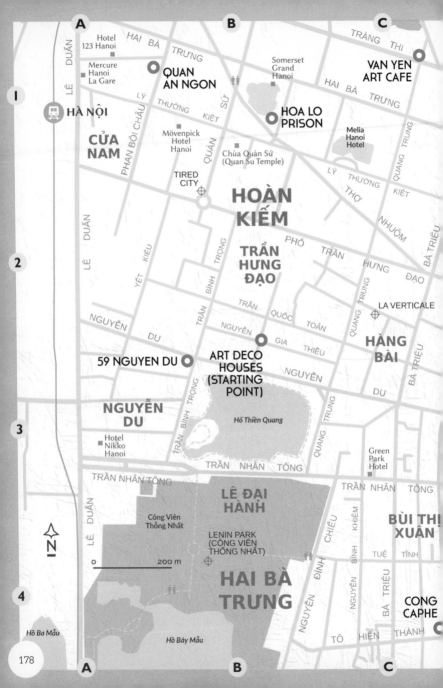

TRÀNG THI

Hồ Hoàn Kiếm

METROPOLE

TADIOTO

MOTO-SAN
UBER NOODLES

Tràng
Tiền Plaza

**REWIND
TEAHOUSE**

HAI BÀ

TRƯNG

**KEM TRANG
TIEN**

**HANOI
OPERA
HOUSE**

**BINH
MINH'S
JAZZ
CLUB**

I

Melia
Hanoi
Hotel

HÀNG BÀI

**VIETNAMESE
WOMEN'S
MUSEUM**
(Bảo Tàng Phụ Nữ Việt Nam)

**INSTITUT
FRANCAIS
& L'ESPACE**

Lan Vien
Hotel

Hilton
Hanoi
Opera

LÝ THƯỜNG

BÀ TRIỆU

**UU DAM
CHAY**

Hoa Binh
Hotel

KIỆT

**RUNAM
BISTRO**

**PHAN
CHU
TRINH**

PHỐ TRẦN

HÀNG BÀI

HƯNG ĐẠO

LA VERTICALE

HÀM LONG

**HOÀN
KIẾM**

PHỐ TRẦN

NGÕ QUYỀN

PHAN CHU TRINH

LÊ THÁNH TỔNG

**NHA
HANG
NGON**

2

**HÀNG
BÀI**

TRẦN QUỐC TOẢN

NGUYỄN DU

PHỐ HUẾ

**CAFÉ
MAI**

**BUN CHA
HUONG
LIEN**

HƯNG

ĐẠO

HÀN

THUYỀN

Green
Park
Hotel

**CHO HOM
(FABRIC
MARKET)**

LÊ VĂN

NGÕ

HƯU

**HAI BÀ
TRƯNG**

TRẦN THÀNH TỔNG

TRẦN NHÂN TÔNG

**NGÔ
THI
NHẬM**

THI NHẬM

**PHẠM
ĐÌNH
HỒ**

LÒ ĐỨC

HÀNG CHUỐI

TĂNG BẠT HỔ

3

TRIỆU

TUỆ   TĨNH

PHỐ HUẾ

TRIỆU VIỆT

HOẢ MÃ

0   200 m

**CONG
CAPHE**

BÀ

NGÕ HUẾ

**CHIM
SAO**

NGUYỄN

CÔNG   TRỨ

TÔ HIẾN THÀNH

VƯƠNG

HUẾ

**MADE IN
VIETNAM**

**ĐỒNG
NHÂN**

N

LÒ ĐỨC

4

ĐOÀN TRẦN NGHIỆP

**VINCOM
TOWERS**

PHỐ

HUẾ

**PHỐ
HUẾ**

179

A   B   C

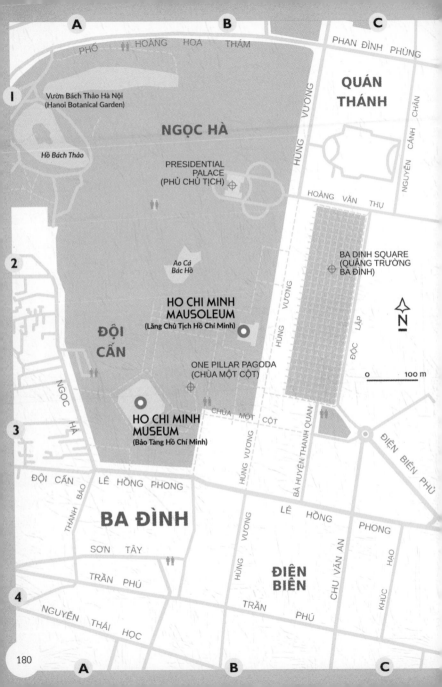

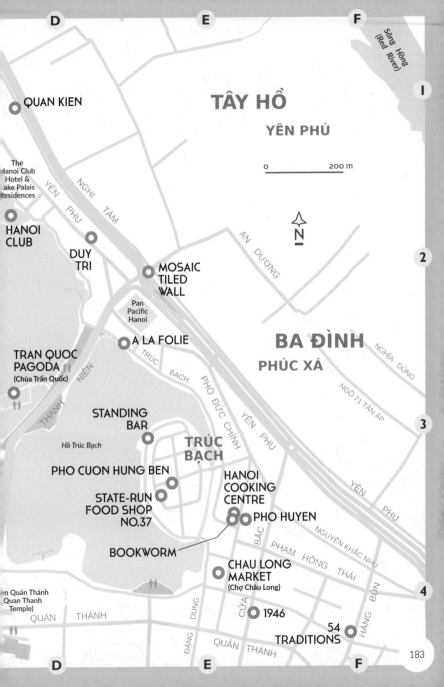

D · **E** · **F**

Sông Hồng (Red River)

1

QUAN KIEN

TÂY HỒ

YÊN PHÚ

0 — 200 m

The Hanoi Club Hotel & Lake Palais Residences

N

HANOI CLUB

DUY TRI

2

YÊN PHÚ

NGHI TÂM

AN DƯƠNG

MOSAIC TILED WALL

Pan Pacific Hanoi

BA ĐÌNH

PHÚC XÁ

A LA FOLIE

NGHĨA DŨNG

TRAN QUOC PAGODA
(Chùa Trấn Quốc)

TRÚC BẠCH

NIỆM

THANH

NGÕ 71 TÂN ẤP

3

PHỐ ĐỨC CHÍNH

YÊN PHÚ

STANDING BAR

Hồ Trúc Bạch

TRÚC BẠCH

YÊN PHÚ

PHO CUON HUNG BEN

HANOI COOKING CENTRE

STATE-RUN FOOD SHOP NO.37

PHO HUYEN

BẮC

NGUYỄN KHẮC NHU

BOOKWORM

PHẠM HỒNG THÁI

CHAU LONG MARKET
(Chợ Châu Long)

BÙN

4

en Quán Thánh
Quan Thanh
Temple)

QUÁN THÁNH

DŨNG

CỬA

1946

HÀNG

54
TRADITIONS

ĐẶNG

QUÁN THÁNH

183

D · **E** · **F**

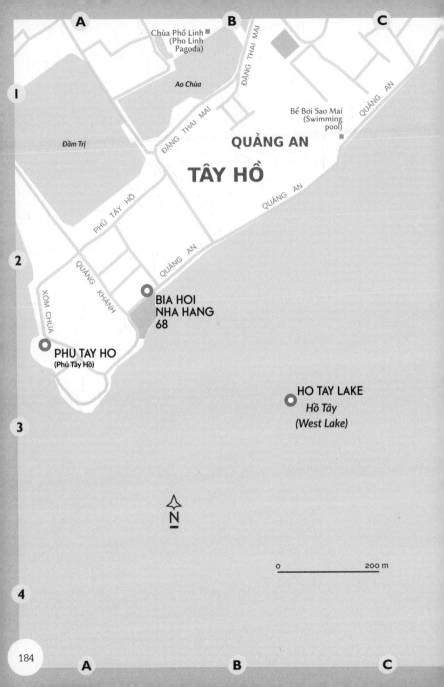

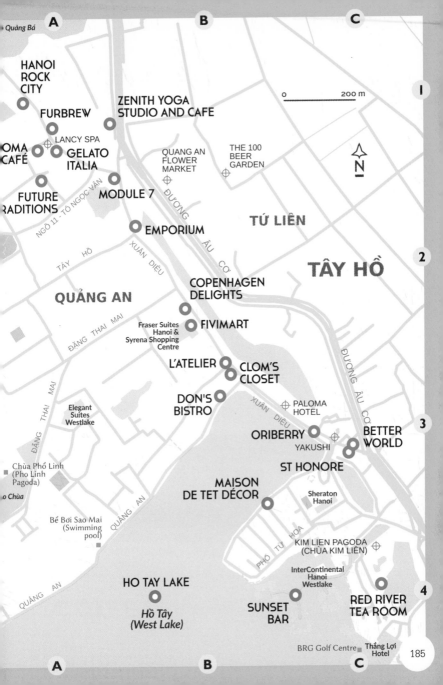

→ Quảng Bá

A **B** **C**

1

HANOI
ROCK
CITY

FURBREW

ZENITH YOGA
STUDIO AND CAFE

LANCY SPA

OMA
CAFÉ

GELATO
ITALIA

QUANG AN
FLOWER
MARKET

THE 100
BEER
GARDEN

N

FUTURE
TRADITIONS

NGÕ 11 - TÔ NGỌC VÂN

MODULE 7

ĐƯỜNG ÂU CƠ

TÚ LIÊN

EMPORIUM

TÂY HỒ

TÂY HỒ

XUÂN DIỆU

2

QUẢNG AN

COPENHAGEN
DELIGHTS

ĐẶNG THAI MAI

Fraser Suites
Hanoi &
Syrena Shopping
Centre

FIVIMART

L'ATELIER

CLOM'S
CLOSET

ĐẶNG
THAI
MAI

Elegant
Suites
Westlake

DON'S
BISTRO

XUÂN DIỆU

PALOMA
HOTEL

ĐƯỜNG ÂU CƠ

3

ORIBERRY

BETTER
WORLD

YAKUSHI

Chùa Phổ Linh
(Pho Linh
Pagoda)

o Chùa

ST HONORE

QUẢNG AN

Bể Bơi Sao Mai
(Swimming
pool)

MAISON
DE TET DÉCOR

Sheraton
Hanoi

PHỐ TỪ HOA

KIM LIEN PAGODA
(CHÙA KIM LIÊN)

InterContinental
Hanoi
Westlake

QUẢNG AN

HO TAY LAKE

Hồ Tây
(West Lake)

SUNSET
BAR

RED RIVER
TEA ROOM

4

BRG Golf Centre

Thắng Lợi
Hotel

185

A **B** **C**

0   200 m

INDEX

ABOUT THE AUTHOR

Juliette Elfick first visited Hanoi in the mid-1990s, when she fell in love with the city's gorgeous fresh food and architecture and the Hanoian appreciation of the city's beautiful lakes. She visited again in 2005 before living there with her partner Brendan and their young son Rem from 2011 to 2013. During this time Juliette wrote travel and lifestyle articles about Hanoi, and worked with the United Nations communications team. Seeing the city from both a leisure and professional perspective gave Juliette a deeper insight into and great respect for Vietnamese culture and people. Juliette now lives in Melbourne where she continues to work both in travel and lifestyle writing and corporate, government and NGO communications. She visits Hanoi as often as she can.

ACKNOWLEDGEMENT/

Thank you to Melissa Kayser and Megan Cuthbert at Hardie Grant, and Kate James and Michelle Mackintosh for your hard work and encouragement on this book.

Thank you to Brendan for taking me to live in Hanoi in 2011 (riding side saddle through the Old Quarter at 2am on the back of your Vespa in heels and ball gown is still the most romantic thing I've ever done). Thanks to Rem for exploring the lanes and cafes of Hanoi with me and charming everyone everywhere. Thank you to Tracey Lister and Andreas Pohl, authors of Vietnamese cookbooks *Koto*, *Vietnamese Street Food* and *Made in Vietnam*, for your valued friendship and encouragement and advice with the book. Thanks too to Cynthia Mann for your work on the book, I couldn't have done it without you. Thanks also to Rebecca Hales, Van Tu Cong and Mark Lowerson, and Nga Hoang and Liem Tran. Hello to all the wonderful people I met in Hanoi; you know who you are. Finally, thanks to the ever-stylish Karan Jones for helping to style and photograph the book.

Please consider patronising businesses listed in this book that support the many social enterprises in Hanoi, such as Koto and Oriberry. You may also consider donating to the amazing Blue Dragon Children's Foundation (www.bluedragon.org), everyday heroes who help children in crisis.

Published in 2018 by Hardie Grant Travel, a division of Hardie Grant Publishing

Hardie Grant Travel (Melbourne)
Building 1, 658 Church Street
Richmond, Victoria 3121

Hardie Grant Travel (Sydney)
Level 7, 45 Jones Street
Ultimo, NSW 2007

hardiegranttravel.com

A Cataloguing-in-Publication entry is available from the catalogue of the National Library of Australia at www.nla.gov.au

Hanoi Pocket Precincts
ISBN 9781741175530

10 9 8 7 6 5 4 3 2 1

Publisher
Melissa Kayser

Project editor
Megan Cuthbert

Editor
Kate James

Editorial assistant
Aimee Barrett

Cartographer
Emily Maffei

Design
Michelle Mackintosh

Typesetting
Megan Ellis and Patrick Cannon

Index
Max McMaster

Prepress
Megan Ellis, Patrick Cannon and Splitting Image Colour Studio

Printed and bound in China by LEO Paper Group